POTTERY GLAZES

POTTERY GLAZES
By David Green

WATSON-GUPTILL PUBLICATIONS/NEW YORK

To Jill

First published in the United States of America 1973 by Watson-Guptill Publications,
a division of Billboard Publications, Inc.,
1515 Broadway, New York, N.Y.

Copyright © 1963 by David Green
First published 1963 in Great Britain by Faber and Faber Ltd.
3 Queen Square, London, WC1N 3AU
Reprinted 1967, 1970

Manufactured in Japan

First Printing, 1973

Second Printing, 1974

Library of Congress Cataloging in Publication Data
Green, David Burnet, 1929—
    Pottery glazes.
    First published in 1963 under title: Understanding
pottery glazes.
    Bibliography: p.
    1. Glazes. I. Title.
TP812.G77   1973   666'.4'44   72-13454
ISBN 0-8230-4217-0

Acknowledgments

In the English edition of this book the help of the following colleagues and friends was gratefully acknowledged: R.G. Barker, T.R. Hare, W. McKay and J. Scott.

The interest and enthusiasm of the students at Bath Academy of Art have helped materially with the preparation of this revised American edition and I am very pleased to be able to acknowledge this in print. The work of many students—and colleagues—is noted in the captions that accompany the black and white and color plates. Among others whose work does not appear, I should like especially to thank John Gaunt, Michael Harris, Jack Pearce, Dinah Rodgers, and Thelma Willis.

Thanks are due in no small measure to members of my own family—Kiki, Jill, and Josephine—for so much typing and retyping, and also to Anne Humphrey for her share.

Several firms and institutions have been very cooperative in supplying photographs or other information and their names are recorded in the appropriate places in the text. At the American Museum in Bath, Mrs. Gonin was especially helpful in providing the facilities necessary for me to take photographs, and John Clark of Carlisle was kind to take such care with the processing of the black and white photographs.

Lastly I should like to express my gratitude to Matthew Evans of Faber and Faber Ltd. (publishers of the previous English edition) for initiating the original negotiations for this new edition.

Preface

The preparation of an American edition of *Understanding Pottery Glazes* — now called simply *Pottery Glazes* — has provided the opportunity to carry out many modifications that have come to mind over the years as a result of various criticisms. I am grateful to Watson-Guptill Publications for their patience in waiting longer than anticipated for these revisions.

Besides a new layout and more illustrations, including some in color, new chapters have been added on devising glaze recipes, testing, applying and coloring glazes, and on the simple arithmetic involved in glaze calculations. The tables now include a full list of the chemical, mineral, and trade names of a wide range of substances used in pottery manufacture. The bibliography has been extended and most other sections have had some revision. The book does, however, remain essentially an introduction to the subject of pottery glazes with a separate section of reference tables that should prove useful to the studio potter.

It is, perhaps, still necessary to say that the very best glazes cannot conceal badly shaped pots, nor are they likely to be the first attributes that you notice on well shaped pots. On many objects glazes are not even desirable, but when they are used with discretion pottery glazes offer a unique range of surfaces, colors, and textures—not found in other crafts—which are immensely exciting to explore.

Contents

POTTERY GLAZES

Plate 1. *This very large crystal of quartz and this smaller one were found at Brandy Gill in Cumberland. These crystals are examples of very slow cooling. Photo: R.P. Wilson from specimen in the Carlisle City Museum, England.*

CHAPTER ONE

The Chemical Background

Pots have been glazed for many centuries; the Egyptians produced tiles with a glazed surface which are said to belong to a period 4,500 years before Christ. It is certainly well known that their knowledge of the art was firmly established by 1500 B.C. The Egyptians were probably the first potters to achieve this distinction, but there is evidence that by 1500 B.C. Oriental potters had glazed some high-temperature wares. At Tall 'Umar on the Tigris, a cuneiform tablet of about the same date (1500 B.C.) has been discovered which describes a pottery glaze.

By the time the Roman Empire had spread to its farthest limits, the art of glazing clay vessels at low temperature was fairly well established in both East and West. Before Romanesque art had evolved into true Gothic, the Orient had produced the finest stoneware and porcelain glazes the world is likely to see. The potteries in Europe and the Near East made their best discoveries rather later. Well before industrialization had taken a firm hold in the eighteenth century, potters in both East and West had produced an extraordinarily rich variety of colored, plain, textured, and decorated glazed surfaces at all temperatures.

For anyone writing or talking about glazes today, it is always sobering to know that such superb qualities were achieved long before the technical aspect of the business was even remotely understood. However, it is obvious that the trial and error methods of the ancient craftsman took a long time to perfect; when there was a break in the line, the tradition was not easily re-established. To some extent, too, older traditions were dependent upon localities; how many of you who would now like to become potters live next door to good felspar deposits or have lead ore outcroppings in your gardens?

The advance of industrial civilization has certainly left its mark on the crafts. The widespread skills of the craftsman have almost disappeared and so, too, that instinctive control of raw materials which defies analysis. Knowledge, by contrast, has increased incalculably. As far as pottery is concerned, there are now a number of people in every country in the world whose energy and enthusiasm has enabled them to take full advantage of this new situation and to bring new vigor to the craft.

What has industry—with the help of scientists—revealed about glazes which could enable a newcomer to pottery to understand glazes more quickly?

Glass

A scientist defines a glass or glaze as a *super-cooled liquid*, but in using such a definition he does not imply that any refrigeration is involved; he means that it is super-cooled *after* its ingredients have been melted.

These ingredients are crystalline. Though it may be easy to see through some crystals, light passing through a conglomeration of them is reflected from the various surfaces and so distributed that your vision is clouded or entirely obstructed. When these crystals are melted a beautifully transparent liquid is formed through which light passes with ease, but in most substances the crystals will reform upon cooling and again reflect the light before it passes through them.

However, there are a few substances which conveniently do not regain their crystal shape upon cooling. Normal cooling speeds are just too quick to allow a reorganization of crystal formation before the runny, molten liquid becomes stiff and immobile. The cold liquid is the same as the hot; it is super-cooled.

How many substances will respond in this way? Written as they are in the list below, it may be difficult to decide whether they are common or not, but one of them is. It is familiar to everybody—potter or not—from his earliest days.

$$GeO_2 \qquad\qquad P_2O_5$$
$$B_2O_3 \qquad\qquad As_2O_5$$
$$Sb_2O_3 \qquad\qquad SiO_2$$

The common one is SiO_2—*sand*—but some people read this symbol as *silica*, others as *silicon dioxide*, and in other contexts the same symbol will be used for *quartz, cristobalite, flint,* or a few other substances.

Chemical Names and Symbols

Confusion can exist, but remember that most chemical substances occur as minerals in the earth and have a mineralogical name. SiO_2 occurs in several different crystalline forms, each of which is regarded as a distinct mineral and is given a separate name such as sand, quartz, cristobalite, etc. Like plants and animals, minerals may have various local, or "trivial," names or special ones confined to a particular industry.

Quite apart from these mineral names the substances which they contain will each have a chemical name, and possibly this will be abbreviated in common use. In this case silica is an abbreviation for silicon dioxide.

Of all the names for a chemical substance only the chemical symbols are unmistakable. They not only describe a substance but are common to all races, even those who do not normally use the Roman alphabet. However, symbols do not help to make a book readable, and the reader will be relieved if, for instance, the word "clay" is used in this book instead of $Al_2O_3 \cdot 2SiO_2 \cdot 2H_2O$. To avoid any confusion, new names will be followed by their symbols in parentheses, and there is a list of chemical and mineralogical tradenames and formulas in Table M on page 126.

The list of glass-formers now looks more intelligible when written out in this way:

germania	(GeO_2)	phosphorus pentoxide	(P_2O_5)
boron oxide or boric	(B_2O_3)	arsenious oxide	(A_2O_5)
antimony oxide	(Sb_2O_3)	silica	(SiO_2)

Elements

The symbols describe many thousands of such compounds, but the twenty-six letters of the alphabet are not unduly stretched, because they only have to refer to a few basic substances from which all the host of other compounds are made. Two hundred and fifty years ago the list of known, basic, and indestructible substances was very short indeed. At that time the list consisted of ten, mostly metals: gold, silver, copper, mercury, lead, tin, iron, carbon, sulphur and antimony, but gradually scientific analysis has revealed others. By 1945 ninety-six were known and in the last decade six more have come to light in laboratories, making a total of 102.

These 102 basic materials of the earth are known as the *elements*, and they are listed in Table C, page 116 in columns of families which have characteristics in common. This arrangement is the result of researches conducted by a Russian chemist, Mendeleev, in 1869, and it represents possibly the greatest single advance in chemical understanding that has been made.

Not all the elements are of interest to the potter. Of the 102 in the full list only ninety occur naturally in widely differing proportions and no more than about twelve are looked for in approximate analyses of mineral substances or potters' materials. About thirty-five, mostly in the upper part of the Periodic Table (Table C, page 116) could be described as relatively common.

Atoms

The smallest part of an element that can exist is known as an *atom*. In enlarged models or diagrams of the inner structure of solids, atoms are shown for convenience as small spheres, but the impression given is false. In fact, atoms consist mostly of empty space and have a complicated inner structure and life of their own which is reminiscent of the universe on the minutest scale.

In place of the sun at the center there is a core, or *nucleus*, consisting of a cluster of particles bearing positive electrical charges known as *protons* and some others bearing no charge called *neutrons*. The positive charges are balanced by a number of *electrons* flying around in orbits and carrying negative charges so that the whole atom is neutral. The distance of their orbits from the nucleus is not great, of course, but by comparison with the sizes of the particles involved it is immense. If the nucleus was magnified to the size of the sun the nearest orbiting electron would not even be as close as the earth!

Looked at in this way, such a mundane thing as an iron bar becomes an object of real curiosity. It is heavy because of the colossal number of minute particles present and it stays in shape because of the efficiency of the electrical bonding mechanism holding them together. Its chemical and physical properties are controlled by the pattern in which the protons and orbiting electrons are arranged.

In all elements the protons and electrons are alike and they are arranged in similar order. The difference between one element and another is caused by the varying number of protons in the nuclei and consequently the number of balancing electrons. In the Periodic Table (Table C, page 116) each element is given an *atomic number* which represents the number of protons contained in the nuclei of its atoms, and the quantity ascends in regular order along the lines. Modern scientists have made the dreams of the alchemists possible; the element mercury (atomic number 80) has been converted into gold (atomic number 79) by the removal of a proton from the nucleus. This was admittedly not an easy or even profitable operation, and the conversion of one element to another in such a manner only takes place under very special conditions. Certain elements, however, whose atoms contain more protons than lead (82) are unstable by nature and ultimately convert to lead by throwing off their additional ones.

The potter is more interested in the chemical behavior of the elements and their stability when combined together into compounds. His attention, therefore, centers not on the protons in the nucleus but on the arrangement of the electrons. These orbit the nucleus in clearly defined layers; a characteristic atom containing eighty-five protons, and therefore eighty-five electrons, will be arranged as seen in Figure 1.

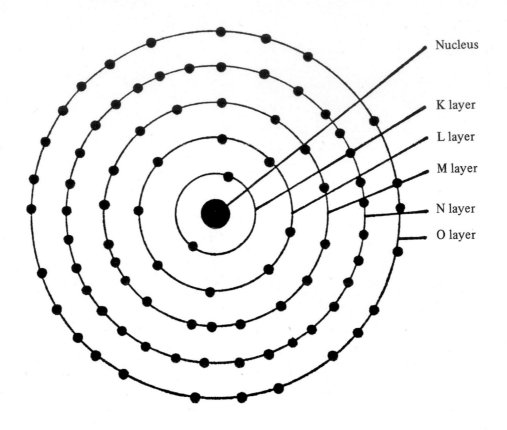

Nucleus

K layer

L layer

M layer

N layer

O layer

Figure 1. *This is a diagram of a characteristic atom containing 85 electrons. In the center is the nucleus. The first ring out from the center (the K layer) has 2 electrons; the L layer has 8 electrons; the M layer has 18 electrons; the N layer has 32 electrons; and the O layer has 25 electrons.*

Forming Compounds

No stable element has, in fact, as many protons and electrons as seen in the atom pictured in Figure 1, but the general pattern for any element can be ascertained from it. The K layer is complete in all the elements except hydrogen (hence H_2), and all those with an atomic number of more than 10 have a complete L layer too. It follows that almost all the elements are going to have one or more complete layers and an outer one which is incomplete. It is this latter layer which gives an element its power and desire to form compounds with selected others; in general, those on the left of the Periodic Table combine with those toward the right.

The combination is effected by an exchange of electrons from the outer layers. Some elements are inclined to free their outer electrons, and others are able to absorb the freed ones into their own outer circuits. The exchange can take place in a number of different ways known as *bonding arrangements*. It is the manner of these bonding arrangements which ultimately controls the characteristics—stability, melting point, malleability, conductivity, refractive index, coefficient of expansion, etc.—of the compound. Most of the elements used in pottery form extremely stable molecules when combined with oxygen.

The electron patterns of the commoner elements are listed in Table 1. Notice that the K and L shells are always filled before the others and that on the Periodic Table (Table C) a new horizontal line commences after each inert gas which contains eight electrons in its outermost shell.

Eight electrons in the outermost shell represent saturation; when elements combine almost inseparable bonds are created when the outer shell of the compound atom (known as *molecule*) contains this number of electrons. For example, atoms of oxygen have six electrons in their outer shells and, therefore, a strong bond is made when an oxygen atom combines with two potassium atoms each having only one electron in the outer shell (K_2O). Calcium atoms have two electrons to donate; therefore only one atom of this element is needed to form a strong bond with one of oxygen (CaO). Aluminium can donate three electrons; therefore, two atoms of this metal contribute six electrons to complete the outer shells of three oxygen atoms (Al_2O_3).

Our knowledge of this subject is constantly expanding and the principles outlined above are highly simplified. Even such a brief explanation, however, reveals the presence of an ordered pattern in nature which commands the utmost respect. The stories of the research into atomic structure conducted during this century are gripping indeed. It is vitally important for mankind that the lessons to be learned from this research are widely understood. Several excellent accounts are noted in the bibliography.

Atomic Weights

As you would expect, an atom that contains more electrons and particles in its nucleus than another atom is heavier. It may be four times as heavy or it may be two hundred times, but because atoms are so small, their weights *cannot be measured* in grams with any accuracy. A weight such as 0.000,000,000,000,11 grams is obviously pure guesswork and of little use in calculations to three decimal places! All you can do with the atoms of elements is to say that one is heavier than another, and patient work has revealed by how much each is heavier than the next, starting, of course, from the lightest one, hydrogen.

In a comparison of this kind it would be reasonable to expect the starting point to be a single unit. With the preceding information about the increase in the number of protons and electrons in mind, you would also expect the scale to increase regularly in whole numbers. However, this is not the case. The number of neutrons contained in the nuclei of the atoms of elements does not increase regularly with the number of protons and is not always the same in two atoms of the same element. Atoms of oxygen, for example, always contain 8 protons, but they may have either 6, 7, 8, 9, 10, or 11 neutrons and consequently be different in actual weight as well as comparative weight with hydrogen. Most oxygen atoms contain 8, 9, to 10 neutrons and their *atomic weight* quoted in international tables (Table B, page 115) is an average of these variants which are known as *isotopes*.

Indeed, early tables gave hydrogen an atomic weight of 1 but later it was considered more convenient to list the atomic weight of oxygen as exactly 16 with hydrogen becoming 1.008. The scale was again changed in 1961 and the most recent figures, based on carbon equaling 12, are given to a single decimal place in Table B, page 115.

Is all this any real help? Surely if you want 200 grams of lead oxide (PbO), you have

TABLE 1. ELECTRON LAYERS OF SOME ELEMENTS

	Shells*						
	K	L	M	N	O	P	Q
	Possible Numbers of Electrons						
	2	8	18	32	50	72	
Elements							
Hydrogen	1						
Helium	2					(inert gas)	
Lithium	2	1					
Beryllium	2	2					
Boron	2	3					
Carbon	2	4					
Nitrogen	2	5					
Oxygen	2	6					
Fluorine	2	7					
Neon	2	8				(inert gas)	
Sodium	2	8	1				
Magnesium	2	8	2				
Aluminium	2	8	3				
Silicon	2	8	4				
Phosphorus	2	8	5				
Sulphur	2	8	6				
Chlorine	2	8	7				
Argon	2	8	8			(inert gas)	
Potassium	2	8	8	1			
Calcium	2	8	8	2			
†Scandium	2	8	9	2			

*Shell N is full after element number 70 (Ytterbium).
 Shell O is never quite filled by any terrestrial element.
 Shell P never contains more than 10 electrons in any terrestrial element.
 Shell Q never contains more than 2 electrons.

†Irregularities found in these elements cause, among other things, pigmenting effects in glass or glazes.

Elements	Shells*						
	K	L	M	N	O	P	Q
	Possible Numbers of Electrons						
	2	8	18	32	50	72	
†Titanium	2	8	10	2			
†Vanadium	2	8	11	2			
†Chromium	2	8	13	1			
†Manganese	2	8	13	2			
†Iron	2	8	14	2			
†Cobalt	2	8	15	2			
†Nickel	2	8	16	2			
†Copper	2	8	18	1			
†Zinc	2	8	18	2			
Gallium	2	8	18	3			
Germanium	2	8	18	4			
Arsenic	2	8	18	5			
Selenium	2	8	18	6			
Bromine	2	8	18	7			
Krypton	2	8	18	8	(inert gas)		

The shell pattern for an element further down the table can be deduced from the figures shown for the elements along the first full line of the Periodic Table commencing at potassium. Taking as an example the column headed by calcium the figures are as follows:

Calcium	2	8	8	2			
Strontium	2	8	18	8	2		
Barium	2	8	18	18	8	2	
Radium	2	8	18	32	18	8	2

only to take 100 grams of lead and combine them with 100 grams of oxygen. If the means to carry out the experiment could be found, the result would be disappointing because only about 108 grams of oxide would be formed.

This is less surprising when you look again at the formula PbO and realize that for every atom of lead there must be one of oxygen. As the atomic weight of lead is roughly 207 and oxygen 16, 100 grams of lead cannot possibly contain as many atoms as there are in 100 grams of oxygen. (This is the old riddle of 1 pound of feathers or 1 pound of lead—which is the heavier?) Let us calculate what weight of lead would yield the same number of atoms as there are in 100 grams of oxygen. Lead is 207/16 times as heavy as oxygen, or 12.9 and therefore 1,290 grams of lead with the 100 of oxygen would combine to give 1,390 grams of PbO.

If only 200 grams of PbO are required, it is quite easy to divide this figure into the proportion of 207:16. Add together the atomic weights of lead and oxygen—223—and the amount of oxygen required for combination would be:

$$\frac{16}{223} \text{ of } 200, \text{ or } 200 \times \frac{16}{223} = 14.35$$

The result of this calculation needs only to be substracted from 200 to give the correct proportion of lead.

This is useful knowledge in forming glazes. Notice how much more useful the symbol for lead oxide is than its name, because the symbol expresses the proportion in which the atoms are combined. The example of lead oxide is a combination of one atom of each element but this is not always the case; in the list of glass-forming substances (page 14) the proportion of metal to oxygen is neither equal nor always the same in any two substances (B_2O_3, GeO_2, P_2O_5, etc.).

Oxygen and a Definition of Ceramics

There is more oxygen about than any other element; about half the weight of the earth, sea, and atmosphere is a fair estimate that has been arrived at by averaging analyses from over the world. The shortage of two electrons in the outer layer of its atomic formation causes oxygen to be more reactive than most other elements. (Fluorine, which is short only by one electron in its outer layer, is even more reactive than oxygen, but there is very little of this element around.)

Since it is known that the earth was once red (or, more probably, white) hot, it is not surprising that such metallic elements as were present at that time in a pure state should have combined with oxygen to form oxides. Few of the elements are ever found in a pure state today. When elements are not in the form of oxides, they are combined with a few other elements which are nearly as reactive: chlorine (giving chlorides and chlorates, x Cl or x ClO_3), carbon (giving carbides or carbonates, x C_2 or x CO_3), nitrogen (giving nitrides and nitrates, x N or x NO_3), and sulphur (giving sulphides or sulphates, x S or x SO_4).

The life of the metallurgical chemist is beset by the curse of separating his metals from oxygen or other elements with which they have combined. The ceramist has none of these problems, because he uses only the oxides of the elements. When he encounters a chloride or carbonate, his kiln automatically sorts out the unwanted elements and sends them up the chimney as gases.

$CaCO_2$ (calcium carbonate) heated gives CaO (calcium oxide) + CO_2 (carbon dioxide gas).

2NaCl (sodium chloride) heated with water, H_2O, gives Na_2O + 2HCl (hydrochloric acid as vapor).

The meaning of a definition of ceramics given by Dr. N.F. Astbury, Director of the British Ceramic Research Association is now clearer: ceramics is a *technology based on metal oxides*. Such a definition covers a wide field of industry, the products of the potter being almost the smallest part. The great brick and refractory furnace lining producers have far more effect on mankind, although perhaps we are not so conscious of their products. The definition is applicable to other materials such as glass, cement, and ferrous enamels. Indeed, in many parts of the world—Britain excepted—industries concerned with these materials are included under the heading of ceramics.

For the convenience of the reader, a list of elements likely to occur in pottery (Table B, page 115) is included, as well as the Periodic Table (Table C, page 116). They contain some information about each element. Notice especially the differences between the melting points of the pure elements and their oxides. Oxides are useful at temperatures well above the melting points of the metals and, because they are already combined with oxygen, are far more stable; hence the growing importance of ceramics in any industry where high temperatures are involved.

Crystals

What happens when the elements combine to give us a compound? The atoms combine to form *molecules*, but the conception commonly held of these molecules being separate within the compound is untrue. When you read "SiO_2" you should not think of a substance consisting of many atoms of silicon, each of which is combined with two atoms

Plate 2. *These enlarged quartz and felspar crystals were found in a fissure in the outcrop of granite at Shap in Westmorland, England. The pink felspar crystal on which the Carlisle City Museum number is written has a volume of about one cubic inch. These crystals are also examples of very slow cooling. Photo: R.P. Wilson from specimen in the Carlisle City Museum, England.*

of oxygen, but as a pattern of silicon and oxygen atoms being present in the ratio of one to two. The pattern is continuous and three-dimensional, so that it frequently reaches an accumulation big enough to be visible, and sometimes so large that a crane is required to lift it. These extended three-dimensional molecular patterns are known as *crystals* (Plates 1 and 2).

If the atoms of a compound are arranged in an orderly pattern, with certain distances and angles between them, then it follows that if this pattern is extended to visible dimensions these angles will create a distinctive shape. Because of this the crystals of one substance are different in shape from those of another, and they can be identified by observation. The drawings seen nearby of common crystals should make this clear (Figures 2, 3 and 4).

Different patterns are obviously going to result in different characteristics and the following further examples of combinations of silica will show this (Figures 5, 6 and 7). Asbestos has a long chain-like structure, often obtaining a length of one yard or more, which is so saturated with oxygen atoms that it cannot burn; it is flexible and may be woven into cloth (Figure 5). Flint is a hard substance and this is a characteristic of all pyramid structures—diamonds too (Figure 6). Mica is triangular or hexagonal in formation, but the pattern is almost two-dimensional and hence its flake-like form (Figure 7).

All this takes time to organize. Heat is required for combination, and the organization of crystals takes place upon cooling. The slower the cooling the more surely crystals will form. The earth took some thousands of millions of years to cool; so it is not surprising that sometimes very large crystals are found. The formation of crystals during the cooling of a molten substance was discussed in relation to glass as a super-cooled liquid, so

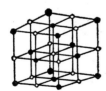

Figure 2.
Schematic diagram of a salt (NaCl) crystal.

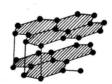

Figure 3.
Schematic diagram of a graphite crystal.

Figure 4.
Schematic diagram of a diamond crystal.

perhaps this is a good place to provide diagrams showing the disorderly structure of glasses for comparison with the previous examples (Figures 8 and 9).

Metals, Liquids, and Gases

What are the other conditions in which matter can exist? In gases, the molecules are disconnected and in constant motion; pressure is the result of these molecules continually hitting the sides of a container. Crowding gas molecules within a confined space causes more frequent hitting of the sides and therefore more pressure.

In liquids, there is a loose connection between the molecules allowing freedom of movement and limited possibility of pressure increase.

In metals, the basic units are not, of course, combined molecules, but individual atoms of elements locked so closely together that the free exchange of electrons becomes possible. When the electrons are caused to move continuously in one direction an electric current is said to pass; other properties which we associate with metals are also due to the intimate contact of the atomic units.

At room temperature (and pressure) most of the chemical elements are solids but they can exist as liquids when they are molten and as gases when the melt is vaporized, although in most cases this latter transformation would require a very considerable degree of heat. The division of the Periodic Table (Table C, page 116) into "metals" and "non-metals" does not imply their state at room temperature. Mercury, for example, is a liquid metal and carbon a solid non-metal, but all the other metals are solids and the majority of non-metals are gases. The "half-metals" or "metalloids"—a group of elements sharing the characteristics of both metals and non-metals—are all solids.

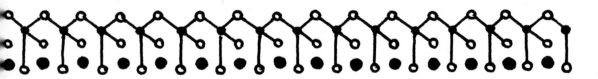

Figure 5. *Schematic diagram of an asbestos crystal.*

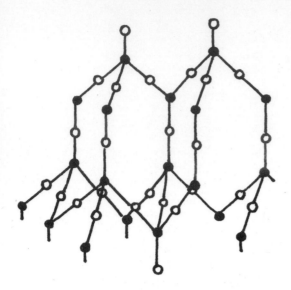

Figure 6.
*Schematic diagram of
a flint (SiO₂) crystal.*

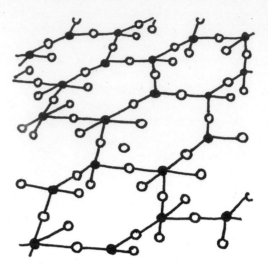

Figure 7.
*Schematic diagram of
a mica crystal.*

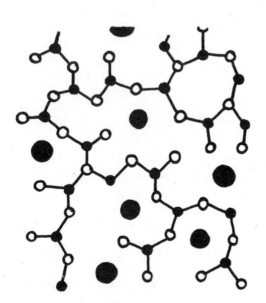

Figure 8.
*Soda glass crystal
with disorderly structure.*

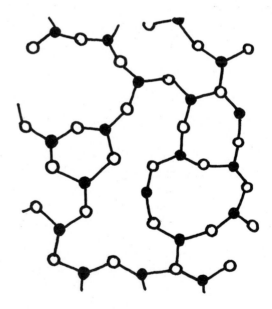

Figure 9.
*Silica glass crystal
with disorderly structure.*

Fluxes

Sand or silica has been mentioned as a possible basis for glass. Why not grind some sand rather finely and spread it over one of your "test", or experimental, pots to see what happens? At ordinary earthenware temperature (1080°C., 1976°F.) or even stoneware (1280°C., 2336°F.), there will be very little change, and when you read that the melting point of silica is 1730°C. (3146°F.) you will not be surprised.

If you can borrow a special, high-temperature laboratory furnace, try your sample in it. However, it would not be the answer because no potter's oven is capable of reaching such a high temperature. If it could, there would be another problem to deal with, because few clays from which the pots are made could withstand the temperature.

A solution to this problem was discovered by the Egyptians. Their sand contained salts of sodium and potassium deposited by dried-up seas, and these metals—or rather their oxides—have the power to reduce the melting point of silica to a usable temperature. Such oxides are known as *fluxes*. There are others which were not found with sand, so that they took longer to discover.

Lead oxide (PbO or Pb_3O_4) is the most powerful of all fluxes and is almost always present nowadays in glazes that melt below 1100°C. (2012°F.). Magnesium oxide (MgO), barium oxide (BaO), lithium oxide (Li_2O), strontium oxide (SrO), zinc oxide (ZnO), and calcium oxide (CaO) also have been discovered to be fluxes. Boric oxide is sometimes included with the fluxes (as in Table 2) but, in fact, the substance is a low temperature glass-former (melting point 577°C., 1070°F.).

The action of fluxes is not fully understood, but it has always been found that simple mixtures of them and silica do not yield a very reliable glaze. Such a mixture is too runny in the molten state, and it tends to melt suddenly.

Fortunately, however, another common oxide which is often found in combination with silica, *alumina* (aluminium oxide, Al_2O_3), has the effect of stabilizing glaze melts. It causes the molten film to remain viscous and in position on a vertical surface throughout a considerable rise in temperature above the initial softening point. Alumina is, therefore, an essential ingredient of glazes, although not necessarily of glasses which are not used in the same way.

The Parts of a Glaze

We have discussed three fairly distinct groups of substances in a glaze, the glass-formers (silica or boric oxide), the fluxes controlling the melting, and substances like alumina which affect the behavior of the melt. For many years these groups were described by names borrowed from chemistry: silica is a mild *acid*; the fluxes are *bases*; and alumina, an *amphoteric*, is something between the two. But recently ceramists have adopted more descriptive terms which refer to their molecular structures. These terms are *glass-* or *network-former* for silica, etc., *network-modifiers* for the fluxes, and *stabilizer* for alumina.

A further set of symbols will sometimes be seen which refer to the important ratio of oxygen to metal in each of the groups, using R for the metal and O for oxygen in this way:

Fluxes	Stabilizers	Glass-Formers
RO		
R_2O	R_2O_3	RO_2

This nomenclature was used in 1886 by the great German ceramic chemist Hermann Seger in a paper which proposed the use of graded mixtures of flux, alumina, and silica, etc. molded in powder form into cones, as temperature-recording devices in kilns. The cones—still sometimes called Seger cones—bend at the commencement of melting (Plate

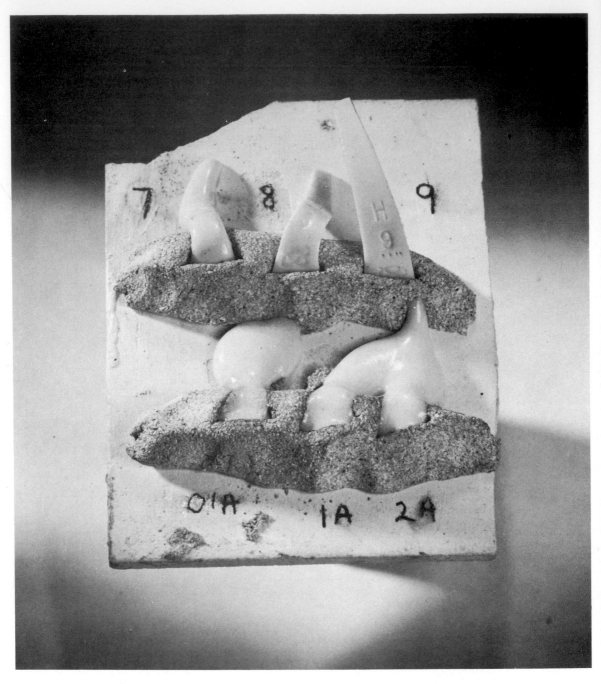

Plate 3. *These pyrometric cones (Staffordshire Seger cones) were taken from a 1280°C. reduced stoneware firing. Photo: L. Powley.*

3) They represented not only a considerable advance over all previous methods of judging temperatures but also in understanding the behavior and nature of glazes. More is said about this important paper in Tables J and K on pages 123–124.

Varied proportions of flux, alumina, and silica then yield glazes with widely differing performances and textures. Transparent coatings over clay surfaces can be created at any temperature between about 600°C. (1200°F.) and the highest point at which common clays may be used (say 1600°C.) (2912°F.) and other surfaces can be formed, which, though smooth, are opaque because they contain a quantity of crystals which have reformed on cooling. Other combinations will reform crystals to such an extent that they are not only opaque but also matt, and it is interesting to note that such surfaces cannot always be achieved in small kilns because of the fast rate of cooling.

Both the opaque qualities and mattness can be destroyed by further heating to complete the melting process before cooling, and all the mixtures can be colored by the addition of other metallic oxides which again form small crystals within the glass (Color Plate 14, page 00). These coloring oxides also have a slight fluxing action on the glass, but the quantity in which they are added is usually insufficient for this action to become very evident in a normal firing. It would be quite impossible to use any of them as basic fluxes in place of the colorless ones listed in Tables E and F on pages 118–119.

It may be helpful to conclude this chapter with a table of the names and symbols of the oxides commonly used in glaze formation (excluding glaze pigments) arranged in order of their functions.

TABLE 2. OXIDES IN GLAZES

Fluxes (RO) Basic Oxides or Network-Modifiers	Stabilizer (R_2O_3) Amphoteric, Neutral, or Intermediate	Glass-Formers (RO_2) Acidic Oxides or Network-Formers
Alkalies:	aluminum	silicon
sodium oxide (Na_2O)	oxide (Al_2O_3)	oxide SiO_2
potassium oxide (K_2O)	(also called	(also called
lithium oxide (Li_2O)	alumina)	silica)
Alkaline Earths:	boron or boric oxide (B_2O_3)	
calcium oxide (CaO)	(A glass-former that has some of	
magnesium oxide (MgO)	the characteristics of a stabilizer.	
barium oxide (BaO)	Presently situated in the R_2O_3	
strontium oxide (SrO)	column in formulas.)	
Others:		
lead oxide (PbO)		
zinc oxide (ZnO)		

Plate 4. *A thin section of the fine crystal structure of basalt (from Arran) is revealed under a polarizing microscope using a magnification x 144. This rock is an example of one that has undergone quick cooling. Photo: British Ceramic Research Association.*

CHAPTER TWO

Geological and Mineral Sources of Raw Materials

Both silica and alumina have been described in the last chapter as being common substances. Of course, sand and quartz are almost pure varieties of silica, but sometimes people are surprised to learn just how much of this oxide is present in other things. It is, in fact, the most abundant substance in the whole earth; it constitutes well over half the earth's total weight. Alumina stands in second place, but a long way behind. The figures are approximately 60% silica and 18% alumina.

However, oxygen has also been stated to constitute half the weight of the world, but in that case reference was being made to proportions of the elements present; whereas in the preceding paragraph the weight of the element silicon has been combined with sufficient oxygen to give the amount of *silica* present. The proportionate list (see Table 3) of elements found in the earth's crust is interesting and shows just how well provided for the potter is.

The fourteen elements listed in Table 3 constitute 99.224% of the total bulk of the earth's crust leaving only 0.776% for the combined proportion of all the other seventy-six elements which occur naturally.

Formation of the Earth

Before going on to see in which mineral form a potter chooses to use these elements, let us consider very briefly how they came to be in the earth in the first place and how the earth was formed.

There are two main theories which seem acceptable in the face of evidence we have. One is known as the *hot earth theory* which suggests that the earth commenced as a vast cloud of white hot gases ejected by the—or a—sun and which slowly condensed. The other, known as the *cold earth theory*, suggests that the earth could be an accumulation of dust particles from outer space which gradually coagulated and became heated through pressure caused by the constant addition of new layers. In either case, it is accepted that the earth was at one time extremely hot and that the inevitable heat loss has been partly compensated through thousands of millions of years by nuclear fission within the mass.

It is recognized, too, that originally the earth did not contain 102 elements. Perhaps, if it was a cloud of white hot gas, only one was present from which all the others have been formed.

TABLE 3. ESTIMATED PROPORTIONS OF ELEMENTS FOUND IN THE EARTH'S CRUST

Elements	Percentage Found in the Earth's Crust
Chief Elements in Pottery	
Oxygen	46.46
Silicon	27.61
Aluminium	8.07
Calcium	3.64
Sodium	2.83
Potassium	2.58
Magnesium	2.07
	93.26 total
Elements of Some Use in Pottery	
Iron	5.06
Titanium	0.62
Phosphorus	0.12
Manganese	0.009
	5.809 total
Elements not Used in Pottery	
Hydrogen	0.14
Carbon	0.009
Sulphur	0.006
	0.155 total

In recent years physicists have broken down heavy elements to lighter ones (A-bombs), built heavy elements from light ones (H-bombs) and deduced that the range of elements we are familiar with, numbers 1 to 102, is only part of a larger range which extends in either direction. Is it not possible that all the original matter has been changed and therefore we know nothing of its nature? The nuclear scientists may provide an answer one day. But in the meantime man appears to know less about his own domain than he does about the space surrounding it. It is easier, indeed, to fire a rocket a thousand miles into space than it is to drill even ten miles through solid rock!

Formation of Basalt and Sedimentary Rocks

We do know, however, that the earth has a radius of 4,000 miles, and that most of the minerals useful to man occur within the first ten or so miles which make up the *crust*. It has been deduced from the transmission of shock waves that the next 1,800 miles is solid rock. Beyond this point it is liquid, with perhaps a solid core of mineral equivalent in density to iron, which is the source of magnetism.

The original crust consisted mainly of *basalt* which is a very hard rock of fine, crystalline, almost glassy, structure which shows that at one time it had cooled comparatively quickly (Plate 4). Basalt is composed of fluxes (calcium oxide, or lime, and magnesium oxide), alumina, and silica (quartz).

Ever since it cooled, or probably even before the process was complete, the crust has been subjected to attack by both physical and chemical forces. Cooling with it there must have been clouds of gases which condensed into water or dilute acids, and since these earliest times the liquids and the solid rock or land have been at war. The rock could not long withstand the grinding and pounding action of the steadily increasing water coupled with the chemical action of the acids, and the first loosened particles of rock assisted the attack by acting as abrasives.

The fine sediment which resulted from this process was more exposed to chemical attack than the remaining parent rock, and it was soon broken down into separate minerals. The calcium oxide (lime) was leached out by carbonic acid solutions and turned into calcium carbonate ($CaCO_3$, limestone), and the silica and alumina combined with the water to form clays, or they floated free. The various newly formed compounds were different in weight from one another and also from unchanged powdered basalt; so moving water soon sorted them out, depositing a heavy material in one place, a lighter one farther on and keeping some in solution.

So layers were formed of different sediments at different places on the earth's surface. As the deposits grew in thickness, pressure was exerted on the lower layers which caused them to change again. The soft clays were compressed to hard rock, the loose silica, or quartz, to sandstone, and the limestone to marble.

Water, acids, and pressure were not the only forces at work on the basalt crust and the new sedimentary layers. As the earth cooled, it shrank, and the crust of hard rock was wrinkled and cracked like the skin of a rotten apple. The sedimentary layers tumbled down the inclined slopes of the ridges; in the valleys these accumulated in thicker, harder, and more mixed up deposits.

Formation of Granite

Volcanic action brought more chaos, and in those early days such eruptions were of inconceivable magnitude. One of the earliest molten rocks to erupt from the interior was *granite* (Plate 5) and it poured out in huge seas from the cracks in the basalt, inserting itself as a blister of molten fluid between this basalt and the layers of sediment already formed. In this position, protected as it was by this blanket of rock, the granite cooled slower than the basalt had done, so that its crystal structure is generally larger and less glassy. Great rafts of granite appear to have virtually floated as a scum on the surface of the basalt and lifted whole continents of sedimentary layers clear above the seas.

It is accepted that the continents have moved since they were first created. Some interpreters of the *continental drift theory* contend that originally there were only two large continents; one around the South Pole; and another north of the equator. Such land masses as South America, Africa, India and Australia floated away from the southern mass, and North America and Greenland have broken away from the northern one. When Africa bumped Europe—before the Mediterranean existed—the rocks were crumbled and piled up, forming the Alps, and when India bumped Asia the Himalayas were formed in the same way.

The granite was inevitably assaulted by the same forces that had already changed so much basalt, and the components of huge quantities of granite were again distributed around the earth (Plate 6).

A time did come when the earth had settled enough for the primitive life cells already in the water to develop, and our certain knowledge of the changes that have taken place in the earth's crust extends little before this time. Life in all its forms has nourished itself from the sedimentary layers and the atmosphere, and it has wrought another series of changes on both. Life has not had an easy passage. Fossils of extinct animals and trees (coal) are often found buried beneath newer layers of rocks 7,000 or 8,000 feet thick.

Active inquiries into all this turmoil have not been conducted until comparatively recently and opinion differs on details. Nothing was known of the formation of the earth until about 150 years ago, and geology is among the newest sciences. The progress has been rapid; already the field of research has been split into three distinct branches of

Plate 5. *(Left) The coarser structure of granite (Concord, New Hampshire) exemplifies slow cooling and is shown here magnified x 144. The striped (twined) crystals are potash felspar; the remainder is quartz and mica. Photo: British Ceramic Research Association.*

Plate 6. *(Above) This rocky debris is found on the edge of Wastwater in the Lake District, England. The action of rain, wind, ice, and the heat of the sun has, over the centuries, broken this mass of rock fragments away from the parent, volcanic rock. Photo: Ivor Nicholas.*

study: *petrology* is concerned with the study of rocks, *mineralogy* with minerals, and *paleontology* with fossils.

The petrologists divide rocks into three broad categories: *igneous*, *metamorphic*; and *sedimentary*. These names are fairly explicit. The igneous rocks—granite and basalt—are those that have come up in a molten state from the bowels of the earth, and, as mentioned, sedimentary rocks have been formed from them. Metamorphic rocks are mostly sedimentary ones that have been changed by pressure or the heat of renewed volcanic activity.

The Composition of Granite

The potter can use rocks of all kinds for one purpose or another, but igneous rocks have a special significance for him. They provide the potter's basic materials.

We have already seen that basalt can provide flux, alumina, and silica, but most of the materials used in ceramics are derived from granite. The coarser texture of this rock makes it easier to break up. If you view a piece of granite through a good magnifying glass, you will see that it consists of three different kinds of crystals. These are clearly defined minerals known as *mica*, *quartz*, and *felspar*. The characteristic dark, plate-like shape of mica crystals is easily distinguished by the naked eye, and often the white, glassy quartz can be picked out from the grayer or pinkish felspar. An average granite contains about 55% felspar, 10% mica, and 30% free quartz with some 5% impurities such as iron oxide.

In total composition granite contains more silica than basalt, and the flux-alumina-silica proportion is such that finely crushed granites sometimes yield satisfactory stoneware glazes without alteration. The Chinese often used such granite glazes and their use has been reintroduced by studio craftsmen today. In his book, *A Monk at the Potter's Wheel*, Vincent Eley gives the following analysis of his local Yorkshire (Charnwood) granite and compares it with a Chinese variety (Kimaichi stone) described by Bernard Leach in *A Potter's Book*. The figures, together with an average basalt, are seen in Table 4.

Crushed granite will not be found in the price lists of prepared materials from potters' suppliers because it varies so much in composition, and it contains a proportion of iron impurities which stain glazes yellow or brown. Such colors may have an unsurpassed richness of quality to the eye of an individual potter, but they are not suitable for the fine-textured, whiteware of industry.

TABLE 4. COMPOSITION OF GRANITES AND BASALT

Minerals	Charnwood Granite*	Kimaichi Stone†	Average Basalt
Silica	61.28%	61.00%	48.35%
Alumina	16.11%	21.00%	13.80%
Calcium Oxide	6.33%	6.00%	10.34%
Magnesium Oxide	4.10%	0.22%	9.76%
Potassium Oxide	3.84%	6.00%	0.58%
Sodium Oxide	0.99%	—	2.42%
Iron Oxide	7.22%	5.00%	11.43%
Manganese Oxide	trace %	0.25%	0.14%
	99.87%	99.47%	96.82%

*Figures from *A Monk at the Potter's Wheel* by Vincent Eley.
†Figures from *A Potter's Book* by Bernard Leach.

Felspar

The three minerals—mica, quartz, and felspar—are easily separated from the very coarse *pegmatite* granites, and the latter two are in great demand for the ceramic industries.

Felspar is a general name given to a group of minerals which contain alumina and silica together with one of the alkali or alkaline earth fluxes. In the commonest variety—*orthoclase*—the flux is potassium oxide and in theory a given sample should include the three oxides in the following proportion:

$$\left.\begin{array}{l} \text{1 molecule of potassium oxide} \\ \text{1 molecule of alumina} \\ \text{6 molecules of silica} \end{array}\right\} K_2O \cdot Al_2O_3 \cdot 6SiO_2$$

In practice, however, the felspar minerals are not clearly separated so that a product sold as orthoclase or potash felspar inevitably contains an admixture of the other common varieties (*albite*=soda felspar, *anorthite*=lime felspar) in its composition. This accounts for the deviation between the actual and theoretical analyses shown in Table H, page 121. There are some deposits where the admixture of two varieties is constant enough to justify a separate mineral name and these are described in Table M, page 125.

The felspars are among the commonest rock forming minerals and most igneous rocks contain one or a mixture of the varieties. The potassium and soda felspars are usually found in the lighter rocks near the surface. Lime felspar, containing less silica, is present in the rocks such as basalt which occur lower down so that basalt contains more lime and less alkali than granite (see Table 5 for typical analyses). The varieties of felspar containing lithium and barium oxides are comparatively rare, but they are included in Table M, page 125.

TABLE 5. THE CHIEF FELSPARS

Mineral Name	Oxide Formula	Proportion of Elements	Temperature of Fusion or Glass Formation
Orthoclase	$K_2O \cdot Al_2O_3 \cdot 6SiO_2$	$K\ Al\ Si_3O_8$	$1220°C.\ (2228°F.)$
Albite	$Na_2O \cdot Al_2O_3 \cdot 6SiO_2$	$Na\ Al\ Ai_3O_8$	$1200°C.\ (2192°F.)$
Anorthite	$CaO \cdot Al_2O_3 \cdot 2SiO_2$	$Ca\ Al_2Si_2\ O_8$	$1550°C.\ (2820°F.)$

Note: Both formulas for each felspar add up to the same thing, and although either may be used, the oxide formula is generally more helpful to the potter.

The molecules of any other oxides differ too much in size to fit into the felspathic arrangement of alumina and silica so we are spared the problems that would be involved if our deposits of felspar were likely to contain an amount of "lead spar" or "copper spar." Indeed this process of selection by size is extremely important as far as the whole character of the earth's crust is concerned and a blessing to many other industries besides pottery.

Micas are somewhat similar in composition to the felspars (Table M, page 125) and, although they are inevitably present in some clays and minerals, they are not used in glazes.

Cornish Stone

In Britain, a country short of economically workable deposits of felspar, a partly decomposed granite known as *Cornish stone* (or Cornwall stone, china stone, or sometimes just as stone) is often used in its place. This rock is mainly composed of orthoclase felspar together with some soda felspar (albite), quartz, and minor additions of fluorspar and iron oxide. Being a rock, its composition varies considerably; it is not possible to give a simple whole number formula, but a generalized one for Cornish stone might read:

$$\left.\begin{array}{l} \frac{2}{3}K_2O \text{ and } Na_2O \\[1.5em] \frac{1}{3}CaO \end{array}\right\} \quad 1\frac{1}{3}Al_2O_3 \quad \left\{ \begin{array}{l} 10SiO_2 \end{array} \right.$$

The flux content is low compared to the silica and the substance was at one time imported in America for use in whiteware bodies and glazes. The composition is very similar to the Chinese stone *petunste* and Carolina stone is of the same type also.

Where recipes specify Cornish stone, a mixture consisting of about 70% felspar (ortho-clase), 20% flint, and 10% china clay could be substituted.

China Clay

Much of the felspar that the earth used to contain has been destroyed by chemical action, but it cannot be counted as a loss because the process has yielded the most important ceramic material of all—clay.

The chemical attack has not always taken the same form. Sometimes it has come gently from above the rock in the form of acid-bearing rain or ice ("weathering"), but at other times it seems to have come more violently from below in the form of acid solutions under great pressure and heat (hydrothermal action). It could have come about in other ways, but the result has always been the same. The flux content and some of the silica has been removed from the felspar, and some of the water which performed the operation remains combined in the new compound thus:

$$\underbrace{\begin{array}{l} K_2O \cdot Al_2O_3 \cdot 6SiO_2 \\ \text{or } Na_2O \\ \text{or } CaO \end{array}}_{\text{felspar}} + \underbrace{xHCO_3}_{\substack{+ \text{ carbonic} = \\ \text{acid}}} = \underbrace{Al_2O_3 \cdot 2SiO_2 \cdot 2H_2O}_{\text{clay}} + \underbrace{\begin{array}{l} xK_2CO_3 \\ \text{or } xNa_2CO_3 \\ \text{or } xCaCO_3 \end{array}}_{+ \text{ carbonates}} + \underbrace{4SiO_2}_{\substack{+ \text{ free} \\ \text{silica}}}$$

The clay formed by this action usually lies near the top of the granite. It is known as *china clay*, or *kaolin*, and is pure white, but not very plastic, because it is rather coarse in texture. If it is still in the same place in which it was formed, it may sometimes be called *primary clay*.

Only a very few deposits of china clay have, in fact, been left undisturbed. The majority have been washed away by rivers or ice floes and redistributed over the earth, collecting on their journeys all manner of mineral, vegetable, or animal refuse. These redeposited clays are known as *secondary* deposits and are almost invariably finer in texture and therefore more plastic, because of the grinding they have been subjected to on their journeys. They do not necessarily collect impurities in transit. In America, there are some useful deposits of pure china clay which have been moved a considerable distance and ground finely but are still quite clean.

The English *ball clays* (Devon and Dorset) are also very fine and devoid of coloring agents, but they often contain a quantity of carbonaceous matter from decayed vegetation which stains them gray, blue, or nearly black in the raw state. These stains, however, burn away completely in the kiln, leaving white clay.

Red clays are the commonest secondary ones. They may contain up to 8% iron oxide, which may sometimes be bleached to a yellow color by the effect of calcium oxide (lime). Other clays appear gray in color, because they are stained with black iron oxide

Plate 7. *China clay is extracted in England by means of a high pressure jet of water. On the continent, and occasionally in America, the clay is extracted dry and mixed into a slip with mechanical blungers. Photo: Watts, Blake, Bearne and Co., Ltd.*

Plate 8. *The glazes on both sides of this test pot have the same chemical composition. The glaze on the left was mixed from the percentage recipe on page 49; the glaze on the right was mixed from pure oxides according to the analysis of this recipe also on page 49. Photo: L. Powley.*

instead of red. Still others contain so much "refuse" of all kinds that they are no longer recognizable as clay; these are known as soils. Table G on page 120 gives typical analyses of various clays.

Most china clay deposits still contain about 80% of unchanged quartz and mica, but these are easily separated because they are heavier. The impure rock is called *kaolinite* or *china clay rock*. It is washed off the face of the quarries by a jet of water (Plate 7); the impurities are settled out in pits as the stream slows down, and it collects in a final tank as more or less pure clay slip.

Alumina

We have now encountered a number of common rocks and minerals that either yield glazes directly or have most of the constituents. Some experiments using them singly or in combination may yield exciting results (see Color Plates 8, 13, 17 and 18 on pages 92–96) especially at high temperatures (1250°C.–1350°C. or 2282°F.–2462°F.). However, none of them are likely to give smooth, clear glazes suitable for fine domestic wares without some alteration to the proportion of flux, alumina, and silica content. To affect this adjustment, the glazer requires other minerals containing only one ingredient in a pure state.

Glazes cannot be prepared from pure oxides, because the duration of an average firing is insufficient to allow the powder grains to combine into a regular—though noncrystalline—molecular pattern. The glaze-forming process is one of modifying an existing alumina-silicate pattern in a clay, felspar, or other igneous rock rather than building one afresh. The truth of this can be verified by using pure oxides (carbonates where necessary) from a laboratory. As an example, the recipe given in percentage of oxides in Chapter 3 has been tested in this way with the result shown in Plate 8.

In this respect glazes are like food. What kind of meal would result from a mixture of chemically pure proteins, fats, and carbohydrates?

Another reason for not mixing glazes from pure ingredients is that one of them—alumina—is only very rarely found in a pure state. It is almost invariably already combined with silica—and probably flux—and, therefore, can only economically be introduced into the mixture by using one of the minerals already discussed. China clay, felspar and Cornish stone are the ones usually used.

The comparative scarcity of free alumina is one reason why it took man so long to discover and purify his commonest metal, aluminum, and also why even today it is still not the cheapest one.

Silica

There is no difficulty in providing free silica for adjusting the proportions of a glaze. Sand, quartz, and sandstone are obvious sources which will spring to your mind, but there is another source which is even more favored by potters and which is easily bought in a prepared state. It is *flint*.

There is some dispute about the origin of these stones, but the majority of flints appear to have been formed from deposits of silica which were dissolved by hot pressurized sea water from the remains of sponges and other siliceous organisms. Flints only occur in association with chalk or soft limestone and are found in abundance in the south of Britain, northwest Europe, and Texas. In other places the process of deposition has resulted in the formation of a layer of a hard rock—*chertz*—which is used for lining grinding mills.

Silica expands irregularly during heating (see page 79). Because of this characteristic, flints and other rocks containing silica or quartz can be crumbled and made ready for grinding by heating them to about 900°C. (1652°F.). This process is known as *calcining*.

Fluxes

In Chapter 1, Table 2 lists three groups of fluxes—alkaline, alkaline earths, and others—which have markedly different characteristics. The metals from which the oxides are derived can be found in the Periodic Table of the Elements (Table C, page 116). Notice that the alkalies occupy the left-hand column of Table C and the alkaline earths the next, with magnesium beside sodium and calcium beside potassium. This implies that magnesium and calcium each have one more electron and one more proton than the two alkalies. It is this addition which causes the three most significant differences between the alkalies and the alkaline earths shown in Table 6. These differences are evident both in their behavior in glazes and the manner of formation of deposits in the earth's crust.

Deposits of both alkalies and alkaline earths can partly be attributed to the same reactions which provided the deposits of primary clay. For every 100 tons of kaolin formed by the chemical process outlined in the equation on page 36, 92 tons of free silica (quartz or sand) and 36 tons of alkali and alkaline earth were released to combine with the carbonic, sulphuric, or nitric acids present in the water causing the reaction. The soluble carbonates, sulphates, or nitrates of the alkalies passed immediately into ocean waters from which they were sometimes deposited when the seas became trapped and evaporated as a result of movements of land formations. The process of deposition is still continuing in a few areas such as the Dead Sea (Plate 9).

TABLE 6. PROPERTIES OF ALKALIES AND ALKALINE EARTHS

Element Group	Reaction of Oxides with Water	Solubility of Carbonates	Melting Point of Oxides
Alkalies	violent	easily soluble	low
Alkaline Earths	less violent	soluble in slightly acid water	extremely high

Alkaline Earths

Calcium and magnesium compounds are only partially soluble in acid waters; therefore, the manner of their deposition has generally been different from the alkalies. Calcium salts for the most part become absorbed into the systems of animals, forming bony structures; later these salts are deposited in enormous concentrations as the animals—mostly of a marine nature—die. The resulting sedimentary accumulation is *limestone*, chalk (sold, after grinding, as *whiting*), or *coral*; the fact that the position of so many sea areas has changed over geological time explains the present situation of these rocks on dry land. Where limestone has been subjected to extreme pressure by an increasing amount of overburden, it has sometimes been changed (metamorphosed) into marble. *Alabaster* and *gypsum* have also arisen through the alteration of calcium deposits.

Less magnesium enters into the bone structure of animals, and though magnesium salts are only soluble in slightly acid water, large quantities of them have remained dissolved in the sea. Magnesium metal is now extracted from sea water by a process invented during World War II when the best ores were in countries under German occupation.

Magnesium and calcium are somewhat interchangeable in the formation of chemical compounds, and many limestones now contain a proportion of magnesium carbonate. Where the two carbonates and calcium have been completely integrated into a clearly defined crystal structure the resulting mineral is called *dolomite*, but where the substitution of magnesium for calcium has only partially been affected, the resulting rock is known as *dolomitic limestone*.

Plate 9. *These salt deposits are located at the Dead Sea, near Sodom in the Negev, Israel.*
Photo: Israel Government Tourist Office.

Steatite or *talc* ($3MgO \cdot 4SiO_2 \cdot 2H_2O$) are other sources of magnesium oxide (often referred to as magnesia) which are frequently used by the potter.

The insolubility in pure water of calcium and magnesium carbonates—together with their widespread occurence, stability, moderate fluxing action, and low shrinkage—makes limestone, whiting, and dolomite ideal for ceramic glazes. Where the inclusion becomes too great, however, the high melting point of the oxides (carbonates break down into oxides upon firing) begins to show, and the resulting glaze may be spoiled. A modest excess is used to restrict fusion of glazes and to promote mattness.

Early in ceramic history limestone was found to harden glazes, making them more durable. In recent years experiments have been conducted on other members of the alkaline earth family—*barium* and *strontium*—with a view toward extending the range of colors and qualities. Both metals are added to glazes in the form of their carbonates, but remember that barium carbonate is highly poisonous.

Alkalies

The relative insolubility of alkaline compounds creates a problem when they are used in glazes, because there is no economic substitute for water as a medium for conveying the glaze powder to the ware. On a limited scale thinned, rubber-based glue has been used effectively as a medium for painted glazes, but costs—as well as harmful smells—prohibit its general use. Soluble glaze ingredients are sometimes mixed with pottery bodies to obtain special effects (e.g. Egyptian paste), in which case they crystallize out onto the surface as the water evaporates.

To overcome the problem of solubility, alkaline fluxes are first melted, or *fritted*, with other glaze ingredients to form a low-temperature glass which, after cooling, is crushed and ground. Then, it is ready for mixing with other minerals to provide a balanced recipe for use at ordinary glaze temperatures. Emptying a frit kiln (Plate 10) is one of the most spectacular sights of the pottery industry, because the molten glaze is poured straight into a bath of cold water in order to shatter it into fragments small enough to be ready for grinding. Modern frit kilns operate on a continuous basis, but fritting can be carried out on a very small scale in a fireclay crucible inside a pottery kiln; the melt can be ground after it has cooled.

There are, however, one or two sources of insoluble alkali flux, such as the varieties of felspars already discussed. Felspars are, in fact, sometimes listed as "fluxes" despite the high proportion of alumina and silica that they contain. However, there is a limit to the amount of felspars which may be incorporated into most glazes for this purpose, because the content of glass-forming oxides is rather high. Glazes high in alkali flux invariably craze (Color Plate 3, page 90) because of the high shrinkage induced by them. The usual procedure is to strike a balance between the very fusible, high shrinking alkalies and the less fusible, lower shrinking alkaline earths.

Nepheline syenite is a particularly useful mineral for introducing alkaline into a glaze, because it contains only one-third as much silica as other felspars. The formula for nepheline syenite is $K_2O \cdot 3Na_2O \cdot 4Al_2O_3 \cdot 8SiO_2$, representing a proportion of one of flux and one of alumina to two of silica.

There is little to distinguish the reactions of sodium or potassium in glazes. Indeed, in most natural substances, the two are often inextricably mixed with perhaps a slight domination of one over the other. Because of this, the chemical symbols are often seen run together as KNaO, or, more exactly as $(KNa)_2O$.

The third alkali, *lithium*, is much less common than the others and, for this reason, has only been used to a limited extent in glazes. It is generally regarded as the most reactive of all the fluxes and can be obtained from the felspathic minerals *petalite* ($Li_2O \cdot Al_2O_3 \cdot 8SiO_2$) or *spodumene* ($Li_2O \cdot Al_2O_3 \cdot 4SiO_2$). The carbonate can also be used and, unlike the other alkalies, it is insoluble.

Plate 10. *Here a molten stream of lead bisilicate frit is poured into a bath of cold water. The molten stream fractures into small nodules which are distributed about the bath by men working with long iron hooks. Before the kiln is empty, the entire tank of water boils with extreme violence. Courtesy James Kent, Ltd. Photo: H. K. Bowen.*

Ashes

Another source of flux, much used by potters nowadays, is the ash left by burnt trees or plants (Color Plates 17 and 18, pages 95–96). The use of ash in glazes was discovered by the ancient Chinese potters as a result of firing kilns with wood fuels. At the high temperature of their firings, ashes flying through the kilns settled on the shoulders of the pots and fused to a glaze. In Europe, where low-temperature earthenware firings predominated, the use of ash was confined almost entirely to the glass industry, though a little was used by the majolica workers of the Renaissance (Color Plate 6, page 91). There is no intrinsic reason why ashes should not form part of an earthenware glaze.

The composition of ashes varies widely from plant to plant, season to season, and region to region. Therefore, they are of little use to the industrial potter whose profits are dependent upon uniformity and exactness of control. To the craftsman potter, however, ashes can provide a source of continual surprise and unending pleasure which—coupled with their easy availability, insolubility, and comparative ease of preparation—makes them very valuable ingredients indeed.

The alkali content of ashes is not usually very much, although it is sometimes high enough to justify their description as a source of these oxides. The silica content is surprisingly high, and the remainder is made up from alkaline earth and alumina, together with minor inclusions of phosphorus pentoxide, iron, and other oxides. Published analyses show variations of between 1% and 16% of alkali (average about 6%); 3% to 90% silica (average about 43%); 1% to 22% of alumina (average 5.5%); and 3% to 90% alkaline earth (average 30%). In general, in vegetable ashes, silica predominates, while in wood, calcium oxide or lime is the major ingredient.

It would be unduly expensive to obtain analyses of ashes; therefore, it is customary to subject each fresh batch to a standard recipe test and to adjust the composition by trial and error after the fired results have been examined. Standard test recipes used by many potters are given below:

Recipe A	Recipe B	Recipe C
20% clay of any kind	50% Cornish stone or felspar	50% clay of any kind
40% felspar	50% ash	50% ash
40% ash		

Recipe C is usually applied like a slip to unfired, leather-hard pots.

If the preliminary test appears dry, more felspar should be added; when the results pool at the bottom of the bowl, the recipe requires additional clay. Some improvement in fusibility will sometimes result from the substitution of wood ash for vegetable ash.

Salt

Soluble sodium chloride (salt, NaCl) is used extensively in the ceramic industry as a glaze ingredient in the extraordinary process of salt glazing. In this process, the glaze is not applied to the ware with water, but the single ingredient is thrown, after dampening, into the kiln towards the end of the firing (around 1200°C. or 2192°F.). The damp salt decomposes with considerable reaction; the sodium content attacks the silica of the clay to form a glass, and the chlorine displaces the oxygen in the water to form hydrochloric acid which is given off as a poisonous vapor. The resulting glazes appear to fall between these limits:

$$Na_2O\ 1.0 \Big\} \quad Al_2O_3\ 0.5\ to\ 1.0 \ \Big\{ SiO_2\ 2.5\ to\ 6$$

The invention of this economical, once-fired process is generally attributed to the Germans in about the twelfth century, and the ware is characteristic of that part of the world. The glazes are coarse by tableware standards, but have a rugged, mottled, and varied quality which is pleasing (Color Plate 7, page 92). In industry, the process is nowadays confined almost entirely to sanitary wares, tiles, or chemical storage vessels, but many craftsmen-potters have taken it up again with enthusiasm.

Salt glazing attacks the kiln interior, the shelves, and the supports as much as the pots, and the process does not work very well until the kiln's interior is well coated with glaze. Alumina is not affected by salt, so that kiln furniture used in these firings should have a high content of this oxide and be washed on the surface with alumina hydrate. Pots should be stood on small pads or heaps of this alumina powder to prevent sticking.

The process is impossible in electric kilns because of the exposed elements.

Lead and Zinc

The other oxides used as fluxes (lead oxide, PbO and zinc oxide, ZnO) appear on the side of the Periodic Table opposite from the alkalies or the alkaline earths and are found in entirely different locations in the ground. Like so many metallic ores, those of lead and zinc appeared as hot "mineralizing" solutions from the bowels of the earth and filled cracks or crevices in already formed rocks. In general, they appeared in sulphide form but the upper parts of the deposits have largely been changed into oxides as a result of weathering. Lead, tin, and zinc often appear together and the veins of these metals may even include enough silver to be worked as ores of silver.

Lead is, of course, one of the oldest and most popular ingredients for glazes (Color Plates 2 and 4, pages 89–90) though it cannot be used at high temperatures, because it begins to volatilize above $1160°C$. or $2120°F$. For many centuries the substance was used in the form of the ores galena (PbS) or litharge (PbO), but the resulting glazes were soft, crazed, and not very durable, and the practice led to widespread lead poisoning. Modern lead glazes contain a proportion of alkali and alkaline earth fluxes, together with some zinc and boric oxide, and the resulting *lead borosilicates*, (properly fired and applied to the bodies for which they are designed) give blemishless, long-lasting surfaces, free from all toxic effects and capable of passing the most stringent hygiene tests.

The problem of lead poisoning from pottery goods has two distinct sides. First, people working in the industry itself can suffer from handling lead compounds; secondly, there is the possibility, discussed later, of lead being dissolved in the glaze of the finished ware if it has been improperly compounded or fired. As far as the people working in the factory are concerned, it was found at the beginning of this century that the danger could be removed if the lead minerals were first subjected to the fritting process used for the soluble alkalies. Turning the lead compounds into a soft glass by this means has the effect of making them practically insoluble in the gastric juices of the stomach. The resulting lead frits (lead bisilicate, $PbO \cdot 2SiO_2$ or lead sesquisilicate, $2PbO \cdot 3SiO_2$) are, therefore, the only forms of lead which can be recommended for use in workshops of any description.

Although the introduction of lead frits brought about an immediate decrease in the fatalities from lead poisoning, much research was needed to perfect them. Early on it was discovered that to be safe, a lead frit needed to contain twice as many molecules of silica as lead. (Therefore, from this point of view, lead monosilicate [$PbO \cdot SiO_2$] is not safe). Rather later, it was found that a dangerous degree of solubility was maintained if the frit included much alkali or boric oxide. The expedient of fritting all the soluble and poisonous glaze ingredients together in one operation had to be abandoned. Therefore, modern *lead borosilicate* glazes are compounded from two separate frits as well as other ingredients required to balance the composition at a satisfactory maturing temperature.

Alumina and calcium were found to decrease the solubility, but since they both raise the temperature required for fritting, they are used in minimal proportions. Fineness of grinding also has an effect on solubility (as well as fusion temperature), so that the lead silicates should be used without further treatment of this kind.

Zinc, in the form of the carbonate, is used in glazes to reduce the yellowness of lead silicates and to improve resistance to crazing. At one time attempts were made to replace lead oxide by using zinc oxide and higher temperatures, but this practice is no longer necessary commercially. Milky opaque zinc glazes (Bristol glazes) are, however, popular with some craftsman potters and the oxide is also used as a basis for glazes in which crystals have been encouraged to grow for decorative effect.

Boric Oxide

Boric oxide has already been mentioned as an important ingredient in glazes. It is soluble but is used fairly extensively in fritted form, because it has been found to assist in the production of smooth, blemishless and craze-free surfaces.

The substance was scarce before the nineteenth century, but in 1857 enormous deposits were discovered in California and Nevada, in the form of *borax* ($Na_2O \cdot 2B_2O_3 \cdot 10H_2O$), *kernite* ($Na_2O \cdot 2B_2O_3 \cdot 4H_2O$) and *colemanite* ($2CaO \cdot 3B_2O_3 \cdot 5H_2O$).

Boric oxide is associated with volcanic activity and hot springs, but the California and Nevada deposits represent the beds of large, dried-up seas or lakes in which the minerals were, at one time, dissolved. It is often thought that the saline waters of these seas or lakes converted the colemanite—which is sufficiently insoluble in pure water to be used without fritting—into borax through the substitution of sodium for calcium. But the two minerals may have arisen as a breakdown of ulexite ($Na_2O \cdot 2CaO \cdot 5B_2O_3 \cdot 16H_2O$) which includes both calcium and sodium oxides in its formula.

The comparative insolubility of the calcium borate (colemanite) compared with the easy solubility of the sodium borate (borax) is further demonstration of the fundamental difference between alkalies and alkaline earths.

Other Uses of Ceramic Raw Materials

In order to maintain some sense of perspective, it is important to realize that the minerals discussed have uses outside the pottery industry. For example, more than half of the world's output of china clay is used as filler in paper, paint, rubber, linoleum, soap, toothpowder, cosmetics, medicine, and cheap cottons. Of all the clays dug out of the ground, the sheer majority are used in the brick industry and much of the remainder in the manufacture of refractories for kilns, furnaces, and cement. Rather less than 5% is used in the whole of the pottery industry.

The alkalies are exceptionally important in every aspect of our daily lives. Sodium compounds—salt being the most important—have widespread uses in the chemical industry and also in the refining of metals, soaps, dyeing, oil refining, bleaching, water purification, and food preservation. Potassium compounds were once eagerly sought for the manufacture of explosives, but now about 90% of these compounds are used as fertilizer. The amount of alkali used by the ceramic industry is too small to show on a percentage basis.

The alkaline earths are similarly useful in the chemical industry; calcium as lime especially is used in enormous quantities in agriculture. Magnesium has important uses in metallurgy, and the carbonates of both metals (dolomite and limestone) are used extensively as fluxes in the extraction of iron and other metals from their ores. The fluxes assist the melting of the rocky part of the ores during their heating in the blast furnace; the molten rock floats on top of the heavier molten metal. The two liquids are separated by tapping from different levels.

Borax has uses as a flux in solders, in refining metals, as an inclusion in metals, in laundry work, soap manufacture, as a mild antiseptic, as a weedkiller, and as a preservative in the timber industry. Certain boron products are extraordinarily hard and heat resistant and are used as abrasives.

Lead and zinc rank next to copper in importance among nonferrous metals in modern industry. About a quarter of the total production of lead is used for electrical purposes and nearly half the zinc is used in galvanizing. Again the use of these ores in the ceramic industry is insufficient to show in percentage tables.

Of all the minerals discussed, only felspar is used almost exclusively in the ceramic industry: one-half of all felspar is used in glass manufacture, and under half in pottery, porcelain, and sanitary ware production. A small amount is used as a mild abrasive in scouring powders.

Geographical Distribution of Ceramic Raw Materials

It would be impossible to mention here all the production centers of the material discussed; even a cursory survey would take many pages. However, the chief centers are listed below and further information can be found in books listed in the bibliography (notably Bateman, *Economic Mineral Deposits*, New York). Detailed information about a particular district is usually obtainable from your local library.

China clay. In England, it is principally found in Devon and Cornwall, Bovey Tracey, St. Austell, and Bodmin; Zettlitz and Pilsen in Czechoslovakia; Dresden and Halle in Germany; Nankan Fu in China; and North Carolina, Virginia, Georgia, and South Carolina (lower grade "transported" clay) in the United States all have deposits.

Felspar. The United States produces about 80% of the total. Other centers, in decreasing order of importance, are found in Canada, Sweden, France, Norway, Germany, Australia, and Japan. The chief districts in the United States are: North Carolina (Spruce Pine district), South Carolina, Dakota (Black Hills), Colorado, Virginia, Wyoming, Maine, and Connecticut.

Nepheline syenite. This is found in Canada (Ontario), the United States, Norway, India, and Russia.

Alkali salts. In the United States these salts are found in California (Owen and Mono Lakes), Nevada (Searle and Soda Lakes), and Arizona (Verde Valley Lake). Deposits also occur in Saskatchewan (Lake Goodenough), Egypt, Germany (Stassfurt), Palestine (Dead Sea), and France (Alsace).

Nitrates. These are located in North Chile (Atacama Tararaca as potassium), California, and Utah (Searle Lakes and Death Valley as sodium).

Borates. These exist in California (Searle, Borax and Owen Lakes), Tibet, Argentina, Chile, and Bolivia.

Lead and zinc. The United States produces over a quarter of the total of lead used in the world and almost half the amount of zinc. Australia, Canada, Mexico, and Russia share about equally the other half of the output of lead; the remainder comes from Germany, Yugoslavia, Peru, France, Spain, and Italy in that order.

The figures for the other half of the zinc output are more equally distributed between Canada, Russia, Belgium, Australia, Great Britain, Poland, Mexico, Germany, France, Norway, and Japan, again in order of importance. The chief deposits of both metals in the United States are found in southeast Missouri (Flat River district) for lead, and the tri-state district of Oklahoma, Kansas, and Missouri for zinc. Tennessee (Mascot, Jefferson City, and Embree) and New Jersey (Franklin Furnace, Sterling Hill) have deposits of zinc. Idaho (Coeur d'Alene) and Utah (Bingham) also have lead.

CHAPTER THREE

Calculation of Recipes and Formulas

The calculations presented here are concerned with changing actual weights or percentages of complicated substances, such as felspar, into proportions of molecules of the individual oxides present in the substances and vice versa. These calculations enable both new glazes to be formulated and old recipes to be compared with statistical tables or altered to suit new circumstances. Without the knowledge of how to do these calculations, the tables of fluxes and ratios of alumina and silica (Tables D, E, and F, pages 118–119) would be almost useless.

The mathematics involved are straightforward, but the multiplication and division can take a long time without some aid. The best help is, without a doubt, a slide rule, and the procedures for using this instrument are outlined in Chapter 8. Slide rules are simple to use and not expensive nowadays.

Methods of Describing Glazes

The following glaze is expressed in four different ways and the calculations provide the means of converting one method of expression to another.

Molecular formulas. Molecular formulas show the proportion of molecules of flux, alumina, and silica set out in this order. For example:

$$\left. \begin{array}{l} K_2O \ 0.2 \\ MgO \ 0.1 \\ CaO \ 0.7 \end{array} \right\} \quad Al_2O_3 \ 0.5 \quad \left\{ \quad SiO_2 \ 4.3 \right.$$

The method is the same as that used to describe felspar or clay in Chapter 2; it indicates to an experienced eye how the glaze will behave at a given temperature.

The presence of fractions in the formula does not, of course, suggest that any molecules or atoms require splitting! The fractions arise because the figures have been so arranged that the fluxes add up to one whole number, making it easy to see at a glance the important ratio of alumina to silica, and enabling this to be compared accurately with other glazes or tables. The usefulness of such an arrangement can be proved by multiplying each of the figures by two numbers such as 30 and 70. When this is done all the figures become whole numbers and retain the same ratio to one another, but comparison of the two sets becomes impossible, even though they represent the same glaze.

The performance of the glaze used as an example here complies with the characteristics noted in Tables D, E, and F and it is shown on the left hand side of the pot in Plate 8 as well as in Color Plate 14.

Recipe for weighing out batch for use. Glazes cannot be mixed directly from molecular formulas, but after a formula has been converted into a batch recipe, it is no longer possible to compare the quantity of constituent oxides with other glazes. For example, both Recipe A and Recipe B below have the molecular formula just given on page 48:

Recipe A		Recipe B	
felspar	111.5 units	pearl ash	64 units
dolomite	18.43 units	dolomite	42 units
whiting	60.0 units	whiting	139 units
china clay	77.58 units	china clay	296 units
flint	150.65 units	flint	458 units

Recipe expressed in percentages. This is the most useful form of a recipe for mixing glazes, because additions of coloring oxides or opacifiers can be added on a comparative basis. The example is the same as Recipe A but here it is converted into percentages:

felspar	26.7%
dolomite	4.4%
whiting	14.3%
china clay	18.6%
flint	36.0%

Percentage recipes also make it easier to estimate how much glaze to mix, for example: 200 grams for a 1 lb. jam jar; 3,000 grams for a small, plastic bucket, and 10,000 grams for a garbage can.

Recipe expressed in percentage of weight of oxides present. Glazes are sometimes expressed in this way—known as the *ultimate composition*—in order to make comparisons. This is not as satisfactory as the molecular formula where the fluxes always add up to one molecule allowing the alumina and the silica ratio to be easily compared:

K_2O	5.1%
MgO	1.1%
CaO	10.5%
Al_2O_3	13.7%
SiO_2	69.6%

Methods of Conversion

The formula on page 48 is again taken as an example to explain how a molecular formula of a glaze is converted to a workable recipe.

Formula to recipe. The step-by-step procedure follows:

Step 1. Draw a table (see Table for Step 1) with a column for each oxide of the formula across the top and a space down the side for mineral sources. The molecular proportion of each oxide is noted in the Table for Step 1.

Step 2. Then, commencing with the potash on the left, choose a mineral such as potash felspar (orthoclase, see Tables H and M, pages 121 and 126) which contains this oxide in an insoluble form, and note it under the heading "Mineral Sources." The formula for potash felspar ($K_2O \cdot Al_2O_3 \cdot 6SiO_2$) shows that one whole molecule of the substance is a combination of one molecule of potash with one of alumina and six of silica, and

FORMULA TO RECIPE, TABLE FOR STEP 1

Mineral Sources	K_2O 0.2	MgO 0.1	CaO 0.7	Al_2O_3 0.5	SiO_2 4.3

FORMULA TO RECIPE, TABLE FOR STEP 2

Mineral Sources	K_2O 0.2	MgO 0.1	CaO 0.7	Al_2O_3 0.5	SiO_2 4.3
Orthoclase 0.2	0.2			0.2	1.2

FORMULA TO RECIPE, TABLE FOR STEP 3

Mineral Sources	K_2O 0.2	MgO 0.1	CaO 0.7	Al_2O_3 0.5	SiO_2 4.3
Orthoclase 0.2	0.2			0.2	1.2
still required	—	0.1	0.7	0.3	3.1

FORMULA TO RECIPE, TABLE FOR STEP 4

Mineral Sources	K_2O 0.2	MgO 0.1	CaO 0.7	Al_2O_3 0.5	SiO_2 4.3
Orthoclase 0.2	0.2			0.2	1.2
still required	—	0.1	0.7	0.3	3.1
Dolomite 0.1		0.1	0.1		
still required		—	0.6	0.3	3.1
Whiting 0.6			0.6		
still required			—	0.3	3.1
China Clay 0.3				0.3	0.6
still required				—	2.5
Flint 2.5					2.5

therefore 0.2 molecules of potash would be provided by 0.2 molecules of felspar. This amount of felspar also brings with it 0.2 molecules of alumina and 1.2 molecules (6 x 0.2) of silica. Now, note these amounts under the respective headings (see the Table for Step 2).

Step 3. The felspar has provided all the potash, but not sufficient alumina or silica and no magnesia or lime. Therefore, subtract the amount it has provided to see how much is still required (see the Table for Step 3).

Step 4. The magnesium oxide can be obtained from an inclusion of 0.1 molecules of the mineral dolomite which would also bring in an equal amount of calcium oxide (dolomite = $CaO \cdot MgO \cdot 2CO_2$ or $CaCO_3 \cdot MgCO_3$) leaving a further 0.6 molecules of this oxide still to be obtained from another source such as whiting ($CaCO_3$).

Both dolomite and whiting are carbonates which decompose on heating, yielding oxides which become part of the glaze and carbon dioxide gas which disappears up the kiln chimney. While the loss of this gas does not affect the calculation at this stage, an adjustment has to be made in the next step by using the molecular weight of the carbonate, not the oxide. The same rule applies to the water content of china clay. When the correct proportion of fluxes has been provided, there remains a shortage of alumina and silica. China clay is the usual source of additional alumina, and flint or quartz the source of silica (see the Table for Step 4).

Step 5. The ratio of the molecules of the oxides has been turned into a ratio of raw materials or minerals. You now need to know the amount of each mineral which could be weighed out to provide this ratio. To do this you multiply the molecular proportion of each mineral by its molecular weight as in the calculations below:

	Ratio		Molecular Weight		Amount Needed
felspar	0.2	X	556.8	=	111.4
dolomite	0.1	X	184.4	=	18.4
whiting	0.6	X	100.1	=	60.0
china clay	0.3	X	258.2	=	77.5
flint	2.5	X	60.1	=	150.3
					417.6

The resulting figures may be weighed out in either grams, ounces, or pounds, and they will provide the correct ratio of oxides.

Step 6. Coloring oxides are usually added as a percentage of the glaze, so it is convenient to turn the recipe into percentages by dividing each figure by the total and multiplying by 100. This can be done on the slide rule very simply. See Chapter 8.

$$\text{felspar} \qquad \frac{111.4}{418} \times 100 = 26.7\%$$

$$\text{dolomite} \qquad \frac{18.4}{418} \times 100 = 4.4\%$$

$$\text{whiting} \qquad \frac{60}{418} \times 100 = 14.3\%$$

$$\text{china clay} \qquad \frac{77.5}{418} \times 100 = 18.6\%$$

$$\text{flint} \qquad \frac{150.3}{418} \times 100 = 36.0\%$$

$$100.0\%$$

Recipe to formula. Any calculation of the kind worked in the preceding six steps should be reversible. There are occasions when it is interesting to convert a recipe by weight into its molecular formula in order to ascertain the reason for its particular qualities, to enable certain faults to be corrected, or to substitute different minerals. The step-by-step procedure, using the same glaze that was used in changing a formula to a recipe, is as follows:

Step 1. Divide the quantity of each ingredient (percentage or otherwise) by its molecular weight in order to find the proportion of the molecules of each ingredient present.

felspar $\dfrac{26.7}{556.8} = 0.048$ china clay $\dfrac{18.6}{258.2} = 0.072$

dolomite $\dfrac{4.4}{184.4} = 0.024$ flint $\dfrac{36}{60.1} = 0.600$

whiting $\dfrac{14.3}{100.1} = 0.143$

Step 2. From the molecular proportion of the minerals found in Step 1, it is now possible to find the ratio of the separate oxides contributed by them. As before, if one molecule of felspar is a combination of one of Al_2O_3 and six of SiO_2, then 0.048 molecules of felspar will contain 0.048 molecules of K_2O; 0.048 of Al_2O_3; and 0.288 (0.048 x 6) of SiO_2. Similarly as one molecule of china clay has the formula $Al_2O_3 \cdot 2SiO_2$ (also $2H_2O$ which are again ignored) the ratio of oxides is 0.072 Al_2O_3 and 0.144 SiO_2. The figures arrived at for all the minerals are now collected together so that they may be added (see the Table for Step 2, Recipe to Formula).

RECIPE TO FORMULA, TABLE FOR STEP 2

Minerals	K_2O	CaO	MgO	Al_2O_3	SiO_2
Felspar	0.048			0.048	0.288
Dolomite		0.024	0.024		
Whiting		0.143			
China Clay				0.072	0.144
Flint					0.600
Totals	0.048	0.167	0.024	0.120	1.032

Step 3. When added together the figures resulting from Step 2 represent a molecular formula, but not one which can easily be compared with others. The standard procedure for making comparisons possible is to divide each figure by an amount which will cause all the fluxes to add up to one whole number. This amount is, of course, the sum of the fluxes as they exist at the moment and the process is called *unifying*. The formula as it exists is:

K_2O 0.048
CaO 0.167 } Al_2O_3 0.120 { SiO_2 1.032
MgO 0.024

Unified, it becomes (as it originally was on page 48):

K_2O 0.2
CaO 0.7 } Al_2O_3 0.5 { SiO_2 4.3
MgO 0.1

Unifying is much the same as finding percentages and can, therefore, be done on the slide rule. The difference is that in unifying the figures are expressed as parts of one; in finding percentages the figures are expressed as parts of a hundred.

Equivalent Weights

Basically, then, glaze recipe and formula calculations depend on the principle discussed in Chapter 1 under the heading "Atomic Weights." Molecules (or atoms) of different substances do not weigh the same. Therefore, to obtain equal amounts of different substances (or the ratios depicted in a glaze formula), it is necessary to adjust the amounts weighed out by the respective "difference factors" or molecular weights.

At times, however, the term *equivalent weight* is used in place of molecular weight. Although the equivalent weight and molecular weight are usually the same thing, there are a few instances where they are not, because the molecules of the minerals involved each include two or more molecules of the oxide which is to take part in the reaction. For example, lead sesquisilicate has the formula $2PbO \cdot 3SiO$. This implies (as seen on page 00) that every molecule of the sesquisilicate introduces two molecules of lead oxide and three of silica into a glaze, and therefore a ratio of 0.5 introduces 1 of lead oxide and 1.5 of silica.

If the method of calculating just described is followed, the molecular weights and not the equivalent weights are used. However, sometimes it can be more convenient to assume that one molecule of lead sesquisilicate introduces 1 of lead and 1.5 of silica and to use the equivalent weight in multiplying or dividing.

With practice, glaze calculations can be done reasonably quickly and although the examples in this chapter are based on theoretical compositions of minerals, not the actual formulas of given samples (see Table H, page 121), they are accurate enough for all general purposes.

CHAPTER FOUR

Devising New Glazes

The ingredients already discussed in Chapter 2, together with many more which are listed in Table M at the end of the book, make possible an infinite variety of glaze qualities and colors. There is much to be gained from devising glazes of your own, starting with molecular formulas. The basic rules of the game are simple enough and sufficient information is provided in Tables D, E, F, and M (pages 118-137) to start you off.

Maturing Temperatures

First, it is necessary to consider working temperatures. For a variety of technical and traditional reasons most studio potters fire their pots between 1050°C. (1922°F.) and 1100°C. (2012°F.) for earthenware or 1250°C. (2282°F.) and 1300°C. (2372°F.) for stoneware. Though the difference between these two ranges has more to do with types of clays or bodies than with glazes, it is obvious that the same glazes cannot be used for both.

Earthenware is porous-bodied, with a glaze lying more or less on the surface, protecting the body from moisture, and immeasurably improving both its appearance and usefulness (see Plate 26, Chapter 7). It is economical to produce, colorful, and, when well made, very serviceable domestic ware.

At about 1200°C. (2192°F.) some—but not all—clay bodies begin to lose their porosity through the fusion of the particles into a more solid mass. When this point is reached, a body is said to be vitrified and the finished product is described as *stoneware*. The production of stoneware involves the use of more fuel and more expensive kilns but the ware has unique qualities—including durability—which makes it very desirable. To some extent the techniques of stoneware can also be simpler and more direct.

Industrial practices involve some overlapping of these broad categories and easy distinctions begin to disappear. Commercial white earthenware and bone china bodies are usually vitrified in the preliminary biscuit firing and softer glazes are then applied and fired within the 1050°C. (1922°F.) to 1100°C. (2012°F.) range of earthenware. Industrial biscuiting temperatures are in the region of 1140°C. (2084°F.) to 1170°C. (2138°F.) for white earthenware, and 1240°C. (2282°F.) to 1260°C. (2300°F.) for bone china.

On the other hand white porcelain bodies are generally fired to an ordinary biscuit temperature (about 1000°C., 1832°F.) and covered with a harder glaze which may mature mature within the range given for stoneware or at a point 50° to 100° higher. A porcelain glaze melting at the 1250°C. (2282°F.) to 1300°C. (2372°F.) range will not be very different from a stoneware glaze and the term "porcelain" is then only indicative of the composition—especially the whiteness—of the body. In true porcelain, fired between 1350°C. (2462°F.) and 1400°C. (2552°F.) or higher, there is not much difference in composition between the body and the glaze as both unite to form a transparent, glassy mass.

The very nature of glazes—their unpredictability—ensures that there are no precise temperatures at which glazes melt. In view of the comparatively simple nature of pottery kilns and temperature-recording devices, you can be thankful for some latitude in this respect.

Melting points can only be defined within ranges. The difference between the point at which a glaze becomes smooth and comparatively bubble-free may be as much as 200°C., although the practical range is rather narrower. A good many degrees after melting has begun, a glaze will still be opaque, slightly rough, and open to chemical attack; the final eradication of bubbles is a matter of time as much as temperature. Some degrees after maturing a glaze will begin to run, although the ultimate point at which it slides off the pot varies with the composition.

Composition in Relation to Temperature

As far as the composition of a glaze is concerned, the chief factor for determining the maturing range is the proportion of alumina and silica included; a suitable ratio can be determined from Table D, page 118. (Many potters have based their glazes upon the Seger cone formulas, selecting one about 100°C. lower than the temperature required, because the temperature quoted for the cones represents only the commencement of fusion.) Most glossy, transparent glazes contain between eight and ten times as much silica as alumina; the brightness of the surface decreases as the alumina increases, so that a matt glaze can usually be achieved with an alumina to silica ratio of one to five. In exceptional cases the ratio may descend to one to three.

The fusability of a glaze is also affected by the choice of fluxes; for instance, the alkalies (K_2O, Na_2O) have a far greater effect than the alkaline earths (CaO, MgO, BaO). Lead is the most effective of the common fluxes and zinc is the least; reading from left to right, the order is given in decreasing effectiveness: Li_2O, PbO, Na_2O, K_2O, BaO, CaO, SrO, MgO, ZnO.

With the possible exception of lead oxide, it is not feasible to use any one of the fluxes singly. They are used in groups with one or another predominating according to the qualities or maturing range required of the glaze. For example, the following are typical groupings for earthenware and stoneware:

Earthenware		Stoneware	
K_2O 0.1	K_2O 0.1	K_2O 0.3	K_2O 0.6
CaO 0.15	CaO 0.2	CaO 0.7	CaO 0.2
PbO 0.45	PbO 0.7	1.0	MgO 0.1
BaO 0.2	1.0		ZnO 0.1
ZnO 0.1			1.0
1.0			

According to the rules for constructing glaze formulas, the proportion in each case is shown as a fraction, with the total adding up to one as explained in Chapter 3.

Tables E and F, pages 118–119, provide some information concerning the utility of the fluxes. Lead ceases to be much use above about 1160°C. (2120°F.). The alkalies and alkaline earths are useful throughout the range of temperatures; generally the alkalies are used in decreasing amounts and the alkaline earths in increasing amounts as the temperature rises.

As a very general rule, it might be stated that glossy glazes fused with a mixture in which the more reactive fluxes predominate will have a higher silica and alumina content than glazes in which less fusible fluxes predominate.

Composition in Relation to Surface Quality and Color

The fluxes also play a very large part in determining the surface qualities of glazes. They also influence the range of color caused by certain pigments used either singly or in combination. This is an immensely complicated subject and, in the context of this outline of the principles of ceramic glazes, full discussion could only lead to confusion.

It is possible, however, to sort the majority of published glaze formulas into several categories according to their predominant fluxes and to evolve broad proportional limits to serve as starting points for obtaining distinctive characteristics. This is rather more useful from the point of view of understanding glazes than a list of recipes or a cataloging scheme that depends simply upon maturing temperatures and minerals. In Table 7, a classification of glazes, boric oxide is again included with the fluxes, because its effects upon physical and color properties are somewhat similar.

Composition of Lead Glazes

Although lead oxide by itself is capable of making a glaze, the result is likely to be crazed and open to chemical attack from acid foods unless it is balanced by at least twice as much silica and some alumina. It has also been found that an inclusion of a small proportion of calcium oxide materially reduces any solubility of lead frits or glazes and substantially improves the glazes' durability.

Most countries in the world have now formulated very strict rules concerning the solubility of fired lead glazes in dilute acids which are similar to those acids contained in foodstuffs. In some countries (America and Britain, for example), it is now possible for local health authorities to obtain specimens of wares offered for sale and to test them. It is also possible for potters to have samples of their wares tested for lead release in order to safeguard themselves. For further information, contact a reputable ceramic supplier and check the books in the bibliography.

A satisfactory high lead (Category 1, Table 7) glaze formula would be:

$$\left. \begin{array}{l} PbO\ 0.6 \\ CaO\ 0.2 \\ K_2O\ 0.2 \end{array} \right\} \quad Al_2O_3\ 0.3 \quad \left\{ \begin{array}{l} SiO_2\ 2.5 \end{array} \right.$$

and such a glaze could be compounded from lead bisilicate, whiting, china clay, and flint.

The addition of certain coloring oxides (notably copper) and boric oxide to such a lead glaze increases its solubility. When the characteristics obtained from such additions are sought, the lead content of the formula should be substantially reduced.

Lead glazes should be fired carefully and soaked for at least one hour at a proper maturing temperature—with plenty of clean air circulating inside the kiln—in order to avoid free volatile lead from becoming trapped in the glaze, which could be released at a later time.

TABLE 7. A CLASSIFICATION OF CERAMIC GLAZES

Number and Category*	Lower Limit of Characteristic Oxide, in Molecular Ratios	Notes
LEAD EARTHENWARE GLAZES		
(1) Predominantly LEAD and without boric oxide.	PbO over 0.5 mols.	Bright fluid glazes with a very long tradition and easily adjusted to fit most bodies. Minor blemishes in application smooth over but care must be taken with composition and firing to avoid lead release in finished wares. Fritting only essential for the sake of the glazer.
(2) LEAD and BORIC oxides both present in significant proportions (lead boro-silicates).	B_2O_3 over 0.25 mols.	Must be compounded from the separate frits (see page 104). Clear glazes with a long firing range and comparatively free from minor blemishes. Modern industrial earthenware glazes are of this kind.
(3) Lead with significant proportions of CALCIUM (lime).	CaO over 0.35 mols.	Lime is used in high proportions at earthenware temperatures to induce mattness. In such glazes the proportion of alumina is high and silica low.
(4) LEAD with significant amounts of ZINC, BARIUM or MAGNESIUM oxides.	ZnO over 0.2 mols. BaO over 0.2 mols. MgO over 0.15 mols.	Generally matt glazes with high alumina, low silica, and no boric oxide. Small amounts of zinc are included in many glazes to reduce crazing and the yellowness associated with lead oxide, but much zinc cannot be used without calcining beforehand. Each oxide has its own characteristic effects on pigments.
LEADLESS EARTHENWARE GLAZES		
(5) Predominantly BORIC oxide.	B_2O_3 over 0.5 mols.	Desirable effects with some pigments but such glazes have a short firing range and blemishes in application do not heel over. Clear, but have a tendency to milkiness if applied too thickly or underfired. Fritting essential.
(6) Predominantly ALKALINE glazes.	Combined total of Na_2O and K_2O in excess of 0.55 mols.	The oldest glazes. Exquisite color from copper, cobalt, and manganese. Impossible to eradicate crazing because of the high shrinkage of the alkalies; fritting almost unavoidable.
(7) Predominantly ALKALINE EARTH glazes.	CaO over 0.55 mols. ZnO over 0.15 mols. BaO over 0.2 mols. MgO over 0.15 mols.	Not common at earthenware temperatures, except for crystalline effects from zinc.
STONEWARE GLAZES		
(8) Predominantly BORIC oxide.	B_2O_3 over 0.15 mols.	Popular "colemanite" glazes.
(9) Approximately equal ratios of ALKALI and ALKALINE EARTH.	Na_2O and K_2O about 0.5 mols. CaO also about 0.5 mols.	Often used for shiny transparent glazes.
(10) Predominantly ALKALINE glazes.	Combined total of Na_2O and K_2O in excess of 0.55 mols.	Color effects as for Category 6 above. Often compounded from nepheline syenite because of its high alkali and low silica content.
(11) Predominantly ALKALINE EARTH glazes.	CaO over 0.55 mols.	A favorite range for matt or glossy stoneware glazes. 0.3 K_2O and 0.7 CaO selected by Seger as a flux ratio for his pyrometric cones and used by many potters since. Most wood ash glazes would fit in this category.
(12) High amounts of ZINC, BARIUM or MAGNESIUM oxides.	ZnO over 0.2 mols. BaO over 0.25 mols. MgO over 0.2 mols.	Very popular among studio potters for matt, textured, and glazes with special color effects. Category includes most "Bristol" and "dolomite" glazes.

*Tables D and F on pages 118-119 utilize the numbers in parentheses on the extreme left to refer to glaze categories.

Plate 11. *Pictured here are Podmore-Boulton Vibro Energy grinding mills and large, heated drying troughs in the factory of W. Podmore and Sons, Ltd., Shelton, Stoke-on-Trent, England. These machines are wet-grinding ceramic materials into sub-micron size. Courtesy W. Podmore and Sons, Ltd. and William Boulton, Ltd.*

CHAPTER FIVE

Preparing, Testing, and Applying Glazes

The bulk of glaze materials do not require much in the way of purification, because most of the "impurities" present in one mineral are as likely as not substances which would need to be obtained from some other source to complete a recipe. In some circumstances the subtle blend of minerals provided directly by natural sources yields a quality which can be achieved in no other way. Industry today can afford to use only pure minerals which are available in sufficient quantities to justify the installation of mechanical handling and quarrying equipment. However, there are many situations where the craft potter can achieve a more individual character in his ware by using the materials close at hand.

As far as the industry is concerned, the chief impurity is the ever-present iron content which is easily reduced by passing all the materials in slop form over magnets, but the presence of this substance is often welcomed by the studio potter.

Preparing Minerals

All glaze materials—that is, minerals—require sufficient fineness of particle size to enable them to react properly on one another. Most of the materials supplied by the trade have been ground until they will pass through a sieve which has two hundred phosphor-bronze or stainless steel wires woven in each direction per square inch; this is called a 200-mesh sieve. Grinding to this fineness is not always necessary or desirable for the studio potter, because materials passing through a 60-mesh sieve may well yield exciting results.

The grinding is done in vast revolving metal cylinders lined with silica rock or (perhaps more frequently nowadays) in lighter machines actuated by vibration (Plate 11). Flints are used as grinding media in the larger rotating ball mills; various shapes of porcelain balls or pellets are available for the smaller jar mills or the vibratory grinders. On a very small scale, pestles and mortars are perfectly adequate and the work can be reduced considerably by heating some of the minerals beforehand and quenching them in cold water. In particular, rocks containing silica—granites, etc.—respond to preheating because the expansion of the quartz content disrupts the total structure.

Water is essential for all grinding processes; therefore you need some means for drying the products off before they can be weighed out. Heated troughs are used on a large scale

(Plate 11) but dry plaster bats or dishes are adequate for studio use. However, commercial materials are not dried off completely because the millers are required by law to include some 2% of moisture in all ceramic ingredients to reduce the amount of dust that rises when it is handled; it is this inclusion of moisture which causes the fine powders to recongeal into hard lumps.

A small percentage of calcium hydroxide is added to all minerals which have been stored in bulk in slop form to prevent them settling to a solid mass at the bottom of the vat; the quantity of the suspending agent is accounted for in any analysis.

Preparing Clays and Ashes

Clays require little preparation for use as glaze ingredients, other than sieving and drying. However, mixing clay until you get a slip ready for sieving can be a time-absorbing operation if the clay is not dried first, smashed into small pieces, and soaked in water for a day or two.

Ashes also require no preparation apart from sieving. Considering the variety and nature of the chemical ingredients from which they are composed, this puts them into a unique position among the glaze constituents.

Some of the alkali content of ashes is in soluble form and is removed by the water added for sieving. (The water can, in fact, become sufficiently caustic to set up severe skin irritation so that rubber gloves should be worn throughout the operation.) While some authorities state that one soaking satisfactorily removes the soluble constituents, others feel that it is necessary to change the water several times before the residue is sieved and dried. Although it does not matter which policy is adopted, there is undoubtedly a difference which is reflected in analyses of ashes and glaze behavior. The presence of much soluble alkali can cause deflocculation of the glaze suspension, making it difficult to maintain a sufficient thickness of the batch. The addition of a little gum arabic to the batch can cure this defect, although too much may cause the glaze to flake off when it is dry.

Preparing Glazes

Mixing a glaze from dry powders which have already passed through a sieve is an easy matter. The powders are weighed out, poured into water, and allowed to soak. After soaking, the mixture is stirred and brushed through a sieve (generally a 100 or 120-mesh) to complete the mixing. If some material remains on the sieve, it should be brushed out into a pestle and mortar and ground with additional water until it will pass through; then the whole batch is resieved to ensure that the addition is properly mixed in.

The water content is now adjusted to an average consistency—one which moves freely in the bucket but only just drips off dry fingers or sticks dipped into it. A batch of this consistency applied to moderately porous biscuitware gives a coating about as thick as a manila office file-folder.

Not all glazes require the same thickness of application. The most suitable coating for any particular recipe or effect can only be found from observing the qualities of fired samples. However, the consistency described does provide some latitude; pieces dipped quickly will take up less than those which are held in the glaze for a few more seconds, and any piece can be dipped a second or third time immediately after the wet surface of the first coat has dried.

The water content of a glaze batch requires frequent adjustment because of evaporation, and glazes need continual stirring while they are in use. To avoid powder settling to a hard cake when it is stored, some potters replace about 2% of the clay in their recipes with the curious clay mineral, bentonite.

Applying Glazes to Biscuit-Fired Ware

The earliest glazes were compounded from soluble ingredients mixed in with the sandy bodies of the wares so that they crystallized out onto the surface before firing. While this method yielded beautiful colors, it could never provide satisfactorily durable and hygienic coatings. Soluble soda ingredients were later employed more successfully in salt glazing.

For many centuries insoluble lead minerals in the form of dry powders were distributed over the surfaces of damp clay pots. It was not until the mid-eighteenth century (in Stoke-on-Trent, at least) that potters began to apply glazes as a thin suspension in water. The majority of pottery is now glazed with liquid suspensions after an initial biscuit firing has imparted strength to the ware and effected a variety of chemical changes; experience has shown that these chemical changes are better completed before the glaze is applied.

With coarse earthenware, stoneware, and porcelain the porous property of biscuit-fired ware is used to assist the application of glaze; the biscuit firing is conducted at a temperature of about 1000°C. (1832°F.). At this temperature the fusion of the clay particles, caused by the melting alkalies, has only just begun to close the numerous pores and passageways through which water can permeate. When clay fired to this condition is dipped into a finely divided suspension of glaze particles, the water (in which the glaze particles are suspended) is drawn into the pores of the ware by capillary attraction, while the powder is left behind on its surface. When the pores are full of water, the sucking action stops; if immersion is continued beyond this point, the glaze powder already held on the surface becomes loosened.

Flocculation

Wares vitrified in the biscuit state (e.g. industrial white earthenware and bone china) are no longer porous and consequently have to be glazed with a thicker suspension, approximately the consistency of a slip. This thicker suspension adheres to the ware by surface tension and must be dried in a current of warm air. To achieve the required consistency for this operation, about 2% calcium chloride or Epsom salts are added to increase the attraction between the glaze particles. This process is known as *flocculation* and consistency is measured in terms of weight per pint; the average for industrial glazes is about 36 ozs.

Advantages of Vitrified Biscuit-fired Ware

The practice of glazing earthenware and bone china on a vitrified biscuit-fired surface developed in England alongside the tradition of enameled decoration. The combination of these techniques is technically and economically sound. Vitrification at the biscuit stage of firing allows the ware to be freely supported in placing sand, or by specially shaped kiln furniture. Faulty pieces can be disposed of before time is wasted in glazing and decorating them. After the biscuit firing, a glaze is applied (much the same for both earthenware and bone china) which is soft enough to slightly remelt during the low-temperature firing of the enamel colors, enabling them to fuse sufficiently to the ware to survive washing up, etc. Low biscuit-firing and high glaze-temperatures with bodies of these kinds would defeat these objectives and in all likelihood would introduce further problems of crazing and other blemishes as well.

Methods of Applying Glazes

Glazes can be effectively applied to ware by several methods, each of which has advantages or disadvantages in a given set of circumstances. See Plate 12 for an example of glazing in a factory situation.

Plate 12. *This skilled glazer is at work at the Wedgwood factory, England. Notice the wire hook attached to his thumb. Courtesy J. Wedgwood and Sons, Ltd.*

For general use on smallish items, dipping is by far the best and quickest method for the craft potter, because it allows the inside and the outside to be treated almost simultaneously. Where larger shapes are concerned—or when there is an inadequate amount of glaze to cover the article at once—pouring can be equally satisfactory. When very little glaze is available, or when the shapes are especially cumbersome, a spray can be used, or the glaze can be painted on with a brush after some siccative has been added. Both these latter methods take time, and, in the case of spraying, require the use of expensive compressors, spray guns, and extractor fans.

No one method in itself offers any difficulties, but it soon becomes evident that some shapes are easier to deal with than others. For instance, one small stoneware bowl with a well-turned foot can be perfectly glazed in a matter of seconds without the need for any touching up; whereas another, of similar size but with a less well-defined foot, may take half an hour by the time various finger or stick marks on the side have been touched up, and in the end its surface may still show unsightly imperfections.

In the production of domestic wares at a marketable price—and with blemishless surfaces—it would seem sensible to take the glazing process into account during the initial planning of the shapes. For example, a properly turned foot can provide both physical and visual stability to a form as well as aiding in rapid glazing. Although there are some potters who would eschew such expediences in their forms, the directness of working method often has considerable bearing on the esthetics of the finished product. With individual items, such as sculptures, etc., such considerations may not apply. Speed is an important factor in obtaining an even coat and success will only be achieved if every part of the surface is immersed or exposed to the spray for an equal length of time and is equally dry at the start. The following methods are recommended for various shapes.

Small articles with wide necks and unglazed bases, or foot rings. Fill rapidly to the brim. Pour out after a brief interval (count to 5). Immediately plunge article upside down into glaze. Hold again; then bring out *at an angle*, twist, and allow to drain. Revert the ware and slide onto the edge of a table (see the step-by-step demonstration, Plate 13). Teapot spouts should be blown down to clear the sieve before the glaze has dried.

Small articles to be glazed all over. Wet fingers in glaze, then hold by your thumb on rim, with your middle finger on the base. Plunge sideways into the glaze; hold for a brief interval, twist, and drain, then rest on a stilt or wire mesh. Immediately dab extra glaze on your thumbprint. Fettle fingermarks when dry (see also Plates 14 and 15).

Medium-sized articles, too large to dip but easy to hold. Fill one or two jugs with glaze. Pour some glaze inside—about one third of the article's capacity—and immediately pour out while slowly rotating the pot. On completion of one rotation the glaze begins to double in thickness; if there is enough glaze left inside for a second coating all around (and you feel this is necessary) continue turning. Otherwise stop and rotate briefly in the reverse direction to avoid the formation of a hard line while the remainder of the glaze is poured out.

Immediately after the interior glazing is finished, hold the pot upside down by the base and twist the hand as far as possible clockwise. Pour glaze freely over the article's surface while rotating back in a counter-clockwise direction. If the pouring is conducted rapidly enough, there will be no mark of the meeting point between start and finish. Second coats should be applied almost immediately when necessary. After draining, revert the article and slide it onto the bench. Touch up fingermarks later if necessary; otherwise scrape and sponge the article's base. Right-handed people tend to hold pots in the right hand while dipping but in the left when pouring.

Large articles, impossible to hold. Few ceramic articles are so large that they cannot be picked up at all and the method just described is feasible for most interiors.

Step 1. Fill the article rapidly to its brim.

Step 2. Pause long enough to allow a film of glaze to adhere to the interior of the article.

Step 3. Pour out the glaze into a large basin.

Step 4. Immediately turn the article upside down, and immerse it in the glaze right up to its foot ring.

Step 5. Now lift the article out of the glaze at an angle.

Step 6. Lightly twist the article to shake off any surplus glaze.

Plate 14. *A small article can be glazed all over if you use stilts to hold it as pictured here. These stilts will prevent finger marks on the glaze. Demonstration: Jill Radford. Photo: author.*

Plate 15. *Another method for glazing a small article all over without leaving finger marks is to hold the object with calipers. Demonstration: Jill Radford. Photo: author.*

However, holding a large pot upside down with one hand while the other manipulates a jug of glaze is a different matter. It is necessary to rest such pots on triangular sticks across a convenient drip catcher such as a garbage can lid (Plate 16). The use of a turntable considerably eases the job; larger drip catchers can be made from sheets of polyethylene when needed. Touch up the stick marks on the rim when dry.

Bottle forms with narrow necks. Glaze the inside of the bottle as you did for the medium-sized article, but to overcome the slowness of emptying caused by the bottle's restricted neck, use less glaze.

For glazing their exteriors, bottle shapes can be held by jamming a stick or brush handle into the neck. Alternatively, you can dip the neck as soon as the interior glazing is finished. Then, stand the bottle on its base on sticks layed across a bucket and be ready to immediately pour the glaze down the remainder of the exterior.

Shallow dishes or platters. Traditionally a platter shape is glazed on the inside only by pouring in a small amount of glaze and swilling it around as near its rim as possible before emptying over one edge. It is possible to judge the amount so nicely that none is left to pour out and no cleaning up is required (Color Plate 4, page 90). A platter which does not facilitate a swill around can be stood on edge over a bucket and glazed by pouring a wide stream from a bowl across its face.

You can glaze the back and front of a platter simultaneously by splitting the stream from a jug over its rim (Plates 17 and 18). Start this operation low down on one side and move the stream towards the center. At this point reverse the direction and start down the other side. To minimize the amount of touching up, most dishes can be rested on two glazing sticks and held by the point of a needle at their tops.

Tiles. Large tiles can be successfully glazed by the pouring method described for dishes. However, it is better to dip a smaller tile by lowering one corner of its face into the glaze and gradually tilting the tile over until the opposite corner has been immersed. Presenting the flat face of a tile to the surface of the glaze batch often results in unglazed patches where air bubbles have been trapped.

When glazing tiles by dipping, pay particular attention to stirring the glaze because the powders settle with remarkable speed, leaving plain water at the surface. Few tiles are glazed on both sides.

Different Colors on the Inside and Outside

Neither of the methods so far described would result in a clean line around the rim of a vessel when different colored glazes are used on its inside and outside. Many potters prefer to obtain such effects by using slips applied to the raw clay, using the same glaze overall. However, it is possible to dip the exterior of a vessel in glaze up to its rim by plunging it into glaze the right side up. You hold the vessel by pressing the fingers of both hands outwards against opposite sides of its interior (see the demonstration, Plate 19). If the two glazes do not quite meet at the rim, this rim can be glazed separately, after the sides have dried, by just breaking the rim into the surface of either glaze. Excellent results can be achieved by glazing all over in one color and then double glazing the exterior by the method just described.

Some types of rims adapt more readily than others to this two-color scheme. You should work out this problem during the initial designing of the form—just as you should plan for any line at which the glaze is to be terminated down the side of a vessel.

Double Glazing

Contrasting glazes, perhaps with wax decoration between them, can produce pleasing mottled or textured surfaces (Color Plate 9). Generally, do not allow the first glaze to dry

Plate 16. *To glaze the exterior of a large pot, stand it on triangular sticks over a wide bowl or the lid of a garbage can. Setting the bowl or lid on a turntable allows the pot to be rotated during the glazing. Photo: W. McKay.*

Plate 17. *You can glaze both the back and front of a large dish or platter at the same time by splitting the stream of glaze over the object's edge. Demonstration: David Close. Photo: author.*

Plate 18. *Here is a closeup shot of the glaze splitting into two streams as it is poured over the rim. Demonstration: David Close. Photo: author.*

Step 1. Hold the vessel by pressing outward with your fingers on its interior and push it into the glaze.

Step 2. Hollow foot rings can be glazed inside by lifting out at an angle. The handle is coated.

completely before the second is applied. The second application should be carried out fairly rapidly so that it is not too thick. However, these precautions are not necessary with all glazes; the most satisfactory combination of coatings and conditions for any particular pair of glazes can only be found by testing.

Spraying

Spraying is particularly useful for applying glaze over elaborate oxide or underglaze painting which has not been fused to the ware by firing. Sometimes this painting affects the porosity of the surface so that a dipped or poured glaze takes unevenly. Spraying is also helpful on plates, bowls, or tiles when a commercial glaze, requiring thin even type of application, is being used. For most purposes spraying is slow and with some forms— particularly those with handles or spouts—it is very difficult to avoid inadequately coated "shadow areas."

Spraying needs to be conducted methodically. Arrange as much of the surface as possible at an angle between 45° and 90° to the spray stream, and move the spray steadily back and forth in different directions until a fur of the correct thickness has been built up. If you concentrate the spray too long at one point, the biscuit will become saturated causing the glaze to run.

The requisite thickness of coating can only be gauged from experience, but different thicknesses can be measured in terms of the fur texture, much as grades of sandpaper are judged by their visual appearance rather than their feel. The coating can be made tougher by adding a few spots of gum arabic to the glaze in the reservoir cup and this practice is particularly useful when respraying over already-fired glazed surfaces. Warming the pot also helps with reglazing.

Painting

However slow and difficult it may be to build up an even coating of glaze with a paintbrush, there are occasions when there is no alternative (Color Plate 1, page 89). Use wide, soft varnish brushes and build up layer by layer, applying the glaze in different directions. Gum arabic or flour pastes added to the glaze suspension help by killing the porosity of the biscuit and making the suspension creamier to work with. Some artists find it preferable to dispense with the water as a medium altogether; they use rubber-based adhesives diluted with appropriate thinners; there is room for experiment along these lines even though the method is expensive.

Touching Up and Fettling

I have emphasized throughout the avoidance of touching up and fettling. However, when there are fingermarks, etc., do the work when the glaze is partly dry. Drip or brush additional glaze onto the bare patches with a soft brush and then shave the glaze down to the level of the bulk of the surface with a sharp knife or razor blade. When the glaze is bone dry rub these patches—and any other minor pinholes or blemishes—with a dry finger.

Dribbles of glaze that run down the outside of an article while the interior is being glazed are a special problem. If the external glaze coat can be applied instantly, before the dribbles have started to dry, they will diffuse into the new coating, but if they are already partly dry when the exterior glazing is started, they will remain as lumps and will require shaving down afterwards. If the dribbles are so bad that they need to be brushed or sponged off, then the pot will need to be dried out completely before the exterior glaze is applied. The hard junction line which results from glazing the exterior after the interior has dried will then need to be shaved and rubbed slightly, otherwise it will show.

Touching up is easy on lead glazes or soft stoneware ones which flow out well in the firing. Matt or opaque glazes of all kinds present a different problem and even the most carefully repaired surfaces will often show in the finished product.

Applying Glazes to Unfired Ware

In spite of the saving in fuel by firing once, the methods of glazing on raw clay are used for only a small proportion of the wares made nowadays. The obvious problem is the rewetting of the partly dried clay during the application of the glaze, but there are other problems concerning the difference of shrinkage between clay and glaze coats in the early stages of the firing and the escape of gases caused by the loss of water, etc.

The difference of shrinkage can be overcome by the use of as much clay as possible in the glaze composition or by exchanging ball clay for china clay in the recipe. Many clays of local origin, which would not be particularly suitable for pot making because of their low melting points, would be especially suitable for use in this way in combination with ashes or even sometimes without addition. A secondary advantage of raw glazing is the ease with which the glaze can be scraped away in lines or patches for decorative effect; the Tz'u-chou vessels of the Sung dynasty are a notable example of work of this kind where even the texture caused by the scraper has been used to advantage (Plate 20).

Any of the methods previously discussed would be satisfactory for applying raw glazes, but, in view of the difficulty of handling the fragile unfired pots, more use is generally made of painting techniques using wide, soft-hair varnish brushes. It is also possible to apply the glaze at the end of the throwing process using the glaze slip instead of slurry from the wheel to complete the forming of the ware. Gum arabic can again be an aid in making the suspension creamier for painting techniques.

Vapor Glazing

The only other means of applying glaze to unfired ware is vapor or salt glazing. The method is simple enough; the ware is packed fairly openly and the firing proceeds slowly because of the unbiscuited ware. You must glaze narrow-necked pots, cylindrical ones, teapots, etc., on the inside first because the vapors do not normally travel down the inside of restricted shapes.

When the firing has reached a temperature of about 1150°C. (2102°F.) any dampers or vents should be closed while damp salt is thrown through special vents which lead to hot spots behind the fireboxes. In all you will need about 1½ lbs. of salt per cubic foot of kiln space before the final temperature—usually about 1280°C. (2336°F.)—is reached. Borax can be used in the same way, or it can be added to the salt in a proportion of about 10%, but it produces a very smooth, shiny glaze, rather the opposite of what any enthusiast for salt glazing would hope for.

The technique requires some experimenting with burner and flue adjustments and bodies. Highly siliceous clays respond the best, and it is often necessary to add flint or quartz to existing bodies before they can be made to respond properly. The body should reach its final stage of vitrification before the last salting of the kiln.

The range of salt-glazed texture, derived entirely from the use of different clays and kiln settings, is enormous, and it can be further extended by the use of slips or coatings of normal raw glazes (Color Plate 7, page 92).

Testing Glazes

Testing glazes, particularly when the recipes are the result of personal effort, is an exciting business. However, it is a job requiring patience and methodical order. Good glazes are often discarded because their qualities fail to show on their first test on a piece

Plate 20. *You can apply a glaze to a damp unfired pot and then scratch out a design. This handsome Tz'u-chou ware is an excellent example of this type of decoration. It stands 13½" high. Sung Dynasty (960-1279 A.D.). Collection British Museum, London, England.*

Plate 21. *Each of the three tests pictured here was done by a different student, but they are all tests of the same glaze. Each student was convinced that he had worked accurately. It is surprising just how many variables operate in the preparation and firing of even the simplest glaze! Photo: author.*

Plate 22. *To prepare color tests, 1,000 grams of glaze are distributed equally between ten jars so that coloring oxides can be added on a percentage basis. The jars are emptied one at a time into the grinding basin; the oxides are then added and ground a little before glazing the interior of the test bowls. Demonstration: Jill Radford. Photo: author.*

of broken biscuit (Plate 21); on the other hand, good pots are sometimes spoiled by the application of a glaze which looked marvelous on a similarly inadequate test. A surprising number of both glazes and pots are also spoiled by mistakes in weighing out or calculating!

No glaze can be described as reliable until it has given good results on a variety of pots in a number of different firings; yet to mix a sufficient amount to use in this way at the outset with every glaze could be very wasteful. A batch of a hundred grams is more than adequate for preliminary trials and the amount should be applied thinly, thickly, and moderately to the inside of small bowls of different clays and fired in different parts of the kiln. It should then be possible to assess the behavior of the glaze on edges, around fingermarks or over slight blemishes or markings on the clay. Then, you can decide whether the glaze has a tendency to craze, to blister, or if it is too fluid. The difference between thinly and thickly applied samples is often very marked; many glazes, particularly commercial ones, behave badly when applied thickly, yet the full beauty of most ash, matt, or opaque glazes is not shown when they are applied thinly.

A glaze which shows sound or interesting qualities at this stage should then be tried on a larger scale, perhaps a 1,000-gram mix applied carefully to some specially made bottles or bowls. Tiles fired flat can give deceptive results; it is necessary to see that the glaze will maintain its promising qualities on proper rims and vertical surfaces. If the results of these second tests confirm the evidence of the first trials, and the glaze continues to behave similarly when thickly or thinly applied, then the glaze can be put into limited use. However, no glaze can be considered reliable or known until it has proven itself repeatedly through a number of firings and over a variety of surfaces.

Much testing is concerned not with the qualities and properties of a raw glaze, but with the addition of coloring oxides to one which is already known to give sound results on its own. Do these tests with equal thoroughness, because the addition of oxides can substantially alter fluidity, mattness, or other characteristics of the basic recipe.

Perhaps the most convenient way of trying color variations is to mix 2,000 grams of the basic glaze and distribute it evenly between ten or twenty glass jars of similar shape and size (Plate 22). When the liquid level is the same in each jar, they will contain either 100 or 200 grams of glaze in each to which oxides can be quickly added and mixed on a percentage basis. You will obtain the most reliable results if each test is lightly ground in a pestle and mortar after the coloring oxide has been added and sieved before use.

Numbering Glaze Tests

Some thought needs to be given to systems of numbering glaze tests because they accumulate with surprising rapidity. One immediate solution is to use the numbers of the categories described in the classification of ceramic glazes (Table 7, Chapter 4), reserving a block of ten or a hundred for each. The first alkaline earthenware glaze to be tested would then be numbered 60 or 600 and the second glaze of this type 61 or 601.

It is helpful to letter rather than number variations on a basic glaze recipe achieved by the use of coloring oxides. Taking the example above, the first glaze might be tested with additions of 2%, 4% and 6% of copper oxide; these tests would then be numbered 60 or 600 A, B, and C respectively.

Numbers should always be painted on unglazed areas of tests with iron or manganese oxides.

Firing and Correcting Faults

Blemishes can be caused on glazed surfaces by a variety of agents and their removal requires an understanding of many processes and reactions. Manufacturers with the best staff and facilities suffer to some extent, and sometimes poorer factories become bankrupt through an inability to produce a sufficient quantity of perfect ware. The potter working for pleasure need not be so worried and some blemishes may be acceptable to him, because they do not make the pot useless or particularly upset its appearance. To some extent industrial wares are so perfect that they are lifeless, but this statement should not be interpreted to mean that blemishes are to be welcomed as the hallmarks of lively hand-made wares! There is a balance between acceptable blemishes—perhaps variations of color caused by flames—and those that are unacceptable; this balance rests with the conscience and integrity of the potter.

In schools or colleges it is probably fair to say that most blemishes arise through lack of experience in applying glazes—putting them on too thinly or too thickly. Others are the result of careless handling of articles between glazing and firing.

However, there is a range of defects which can be directly traced to the composition of the glaze, its individual constituents, or to the firing of the ware. Some steps which can be taken to overcome them are outlined in the following pages.

Crazing

The usual explanation of crazing is that the glaze does not fit the clay so that cracks appear when it cools. The impression gained from this is that the two—clay and glaze—must expand and shrink alike, but that is not quite a sufficient explanation. In order to prevent crazing, the glaze film must be a little *larger* than the pot so that it is under slight compression.

If the glaze shrinks more than the pot, then the glaze is stretched and is almost certain to craze. In comparison with most materials, glazes can stand up to compressing to a far greater extent than they can withstand the forces of tension or stretching. In order to achieve a state of compression in the glaze, it is necessary to see that the clay continues to shrink after the glaze coat has established its final size.

What Happens During Firing?

Most substances expand when heated and contract when cooled, but in the firing of any clay goods this reaction is complicated by various chemical and physical changes. At 100°C. (212°F.) the water which was mixed with the clay to make it plastic is driven away. Although the shrinkage that accompanies this loss has already taken place before the commencement of the firing, a little moisture inevitably remains trapped within the interstices of the clay particles until heat is applied.

Between 450°C. (842°F.) and 500°C. (932°F.) the water shown in the clay formula ($Al_2O_3 \cdot 2SiO_2 \cdot 2H_2O$) is dislodged leaving the mineral *metakaolin*, somewhat larger in its crystal size than the original *kaolin*; therefore, the change is accompanied by expansion. This alteration represents, of course, the point at which clay changes to pottery and in any ordinary circumstances it is irreversible.

At temperatures between 500°C. (932°F.) and 800°C. (1472°F.) carbonaceous matter in the clay is oxidized away and any carbonates, chlorides, or fluorides break down with the evolution of the respective gases and some shrinkage. At the same time the alkalies begin to melt and to sinter, or fuse, the edges of the clay particles, forming a glassy bond which increases in amount as the firing proceeds, reducing still further the volume of the clay mass.

At about 1000°C. (1832°F.) any sulphides included in the composition of the clay break into oxides and sulphur dioxide. This finally rids the clay of any combustible content, and the clay itself begins to undergo a further change of crystal structure. As far as the curing of crazing is concerned, this latter change in the crystal structure of the clay is vital, because an amount of silica is freed which will suddenly contract during the last stage of cooling, long after the glaze has set and assumed its final size of coating.

Changes in Silica During Firing

Silica is known to exist in at least six different crystalline arrangements, and one pattern may be changed into another by heat or pressure. Some of the patterns require more space than others; so conversion is accompanied by an increase in volume, and reversion is accomplished during cooling by a decrease. What is thought to happen at 1000°C. (1832°F.) is that the metakaolin molecules formed earlier start to change into the mineral *mullite* which requires only a third as much silica in its crystalline network. The remaining two-thirds of the silica are set free as quartz which also undergoes a change of structure to the form of silica known as *cristobalite*, thus:

$3Al_2O_3 \cdot 6SiO_2$ (3 molecules of metakaolin) at 1000°C. (1832°F.) becomes
$3Al_2O_3 \cdot 2SiO_2$ (1 molecule of mullite) + $4SiO_2$ (4 molecules of silica or quartz)

At 220°C. (428°F.) during the cooling, the "beta" type of cristobalite formed earlier reverts to the form of "alpha" cristobalite with a decrease of volume of 3%; therefore, the glaze is put into compression at this point. The reaction is known rather amusingly as the "cristobalite squeeze."

If the temperature of the biscuit or glaze firing is to be less than the 1100°C. (2012°F.) required to complete the formation of mullite, some shrinkage can be arranged after the glaze has set by adding flint to the clay body. At temperatures between 550°C. (1022°F.) and 600°C. (1112°F.) the flint changes from the standard "alpha quartz" type of structure to "beta quartz" with an expansion of about 1% (see Figures 10 and 11). During cooling past this temperature range, shrinkage again takes place on the reversion of the beta quartz to alpha quartz with corresponding compressive action on the glaze.

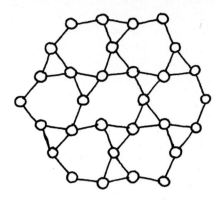

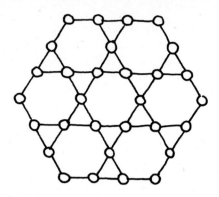

Figure 10. *At temperatures up to 575°C. (1047°F.) flint has the standard alpha quartz type of structure pictured here.*

Figure 11. *At temperatures over 575°C. (1047°F.) the alpha quartz structure changes to the beta quartz structure seen in this diagram.*

How to Avoid Crazing

If it is not possible to add flint to the clay—not light work in any case—then the only other course to reduce crazing is to alter the contraction of the glaze itself by changing its composition. The poor record of the alkalies in terms of causing contraction and subsequent crazing has already been mentioned. The obvious solution is to reduce the proportion of them in the recipe. This can be done either by a straight swap of fluxes, exchanging perhaps alkali for zinc which is sometimes called the "anti-craze," or by increasing the ratio of glass-formers by the addition of borax or silica.

It may seem strange that crazing can be cured by the addition of the same substance to the glaze or to the body, but the reasons are quite different. There is no question of cristobalite being formed within the glaze where the melting action, which only just begins in the clay body, is entirely completed. The silica content of a glaze cannot, however, be increased without restriction and an exchange of about 5% of alkali-bearing felspar for flint is about the most that could be tolerated in many compositions.

Alteration of the glaze may not be a permanent answer, because in domestic use clay bodies which are still porous expand as they absorb water. The amount of expansion may well be sufficient to change the force on the glaze from compression to tension. With properly vitrified stoneware or porcelain, water absorption should not take place.

Firing Schedules

Clay shrinks and expands several times during firing; therefore, it follows that the process should not be conducted too rapidly. The chemical changes involved are much slower than most of the reactions conducted with liquids and powders in a laboratory. The physical changes of crystalline form—particularly the change from quartz to crystobalite—take considerable time to complete themselves throughout the mass. A rise of temperature of between 60°C. (140°F.) and 100°C. (212°F.) per hour is reasonable for biscuit firing provided the final temperature is held by soaking for an hour or more. Glaze firings can proceed at up to 150°C. (302°F.) per hour because there is no longer any combustible matter in the clay that must be removed. Again, soaking for one or two hours has an appreciable effect on the quality of the finished ware (see Plates 23 A–D).

Plate 23. *In the four enlarged photographs above, a transparent lead borosilicate glaze is seen at various stages of firing. The vertical line through the center of each photo is caused by a platinum wire .003 inches in diameter which has been embedded in the glaze to give a comparative scale. Photo: British Ceramic Research Association.*

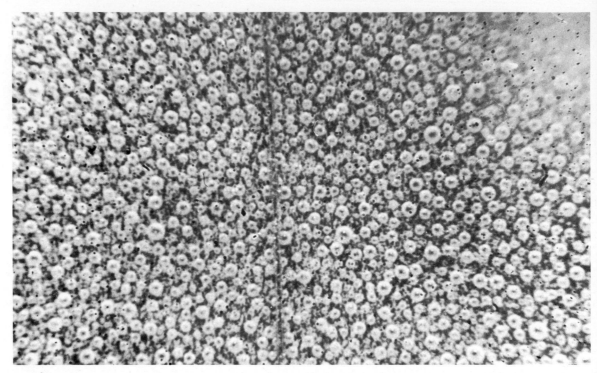

1030°C.

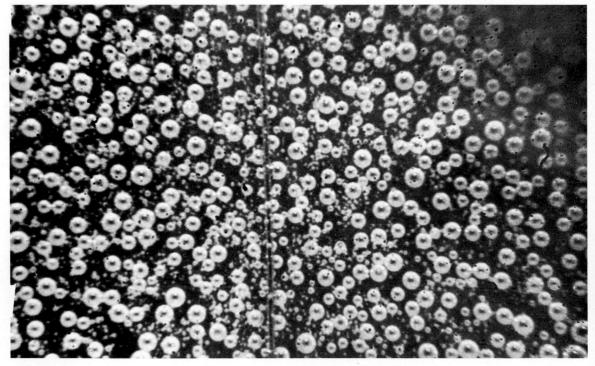

1070°C.

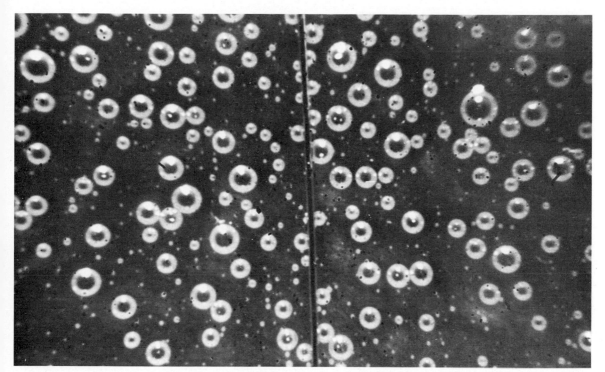

1100°C.

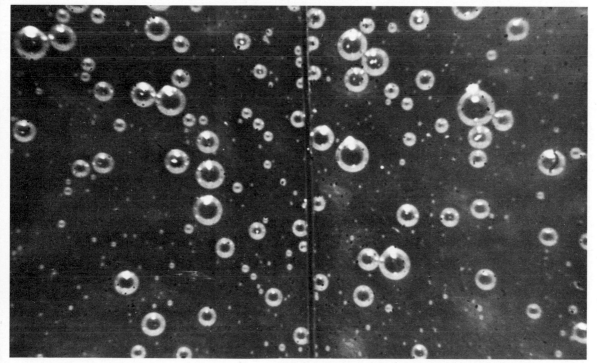

1100°C. after four hours of soaking.

There is a real risk of shattering ware during any of the changes; therefore a recapitulation of the danger points may be helpful:

100°C. (212°F.). Any remaining "water of plasticity" is driven off; immediate shrinkage.

450°C.-500°C. (842°F.-932°F.). "Water of formation" is driven away (about 450 cu. ft. of steam for each hundredweight of clay goods). Expansion follows the formation of metakaolin.

500°C.-800°C. (932°F.-1472°F.). Carbonaceous matter oxidizes; carbonates, chlorides, and fluorides break down. Each change is accompanied by the liberation of gas and shrinkage. (Remember, it is important to have adequate ventilation around electric kilns during this part of the firing, because some of the gases evolved are poisonous. In gas kilns that use oil, or solid fuels, the gases generally escape up the chimney.)

800°C. (1472°F.). Alkalies start the process of vitrification involving shrinkage.

1000°C. (1832°F.). Metakaolin changes to mullite leaving some silica free to convert to alpha cristobalite. Conversion involves expansion.

1100°C. (2012°F.). After some soaking, the change to cristobalite will have proceeded as far as possible.

Cooling. 900°C.-800°C. (1652°F.-1472°F.). During cooling there are three points to watch: slow cooling between these temperatures encourages the growth of crystals in glazes; noncrystalline glossy glazes should be cooled rapidly down to 700°C. (1292°F.).

600°C.-550°C. (1112°F.-1022°F.). Reversion of beta quartz to alpha quartz. 1% shrinkage.

220°C. (428°F.). Reversion of beta cristobalite to alpha cristobalite. 3% shrinkage.

Peeling or Flaking

Peeling of the glaze—especially on the rims of pots—is caused by the reverse of the mechanism that causes crazing. When peeling occurs, the glaze is far too large for the clay, but this happens less frequently, because it is a matter of too much compression rather than tension. Two cures for this are the reverse of those for crazing; either fire at a lower temperature; or add some alkali flux to the glaze which will increase the shrinkage.

Peeling happens most often on stoneware pots. Lowering the firing temperature will have no effect on stoneware due to the fact that the temperature is well above that required to free quartz; the only cure here is to soften the glaze with more flux.

Crawling

Occasionally glazes roll up in lumps leaving bare patches of clay; there are a number of causes for this. The commonest cause is that the glaze coating was not properly attached to the biscuit-fired ware in the first place, either because the biscuit was dusty, greasy, or because the glaze was too powdery. Crawling often occurs also when the glaze film is rewetted by twice dipping; when it is too thick; or when it is disturbed by some additional decorative work, especially wax resist. In the case of an undamaged glaze film, crawling occurs after large blisters have appeared during the early heating, causing gaps which are too wide to heal over.

If none of these causes is suspected, the trouble may be in the composition of the glaze itself. Opaque glazes are particularly prone to crawl when they are applied too thickly, because the large percentage of opacifier involved causes them to be slightly infusible. If the glaze is leadless, the crawling is even more likely to occur, because lead glazes are more fluid than most others at their maturing temperature.

A fluid glaze is less prone to crawl. The cure, then, for a glaze that does crawl is to make it more fluid by adding additional flux. The difficulty with opaque glazes is that the additional flux tends to dissolve the opacifier, but a slightly thicker coat may be effective.

Another cause of crawling has already been mentioned. It occurs when too much volatile matter in the form of combined gases or water (as in clay) is incorporated into the glaze. When this occurs, there is not enough of the glaze left to cover the pot when the volatile matter has gone. This particularly affects glazes made from "local" raw materials or ashes, and it can be eradicated by first heating some of them to about 850°C. (1562°F.) before they are incorporated into the mixture. You sometimes come across recipes containing an exceptional amount of china clay; these recipes specify that half of the quantity of china clay should be calcined before use.

Pinholing

Pinholing may arise from a number of causes, including some of those already mentioned for crawling, such as dusty biscuitware or faulty application of glaze.

Most pinholes, however, are caused by the escape of gases released by the breakdown of carbonates, clays, etc. in the body of the glaze, or by the escape of steam from the water used in glazing. Care in firing, especially soaking at the end of the process, is essential. This is brought out very clearly in a remarkable film of a glaze being fired produced by the British Ceramic Research Association, from which the photos that comprise Plate 23 are taken. In this film a small area of glaze is enlarged to fill a cinema screen. Between 950°C. (1742°F.) and 1050°C. (1922°F.) reaction is visible; minute beads of glass form which gradually combine to create larger ones. Some of the beads are, in fact, blisters caused by escaping gases from the glazes or air from the pores of the pot. The blisters burst leaving craters, but towards 1080° (1976°F.) both beads and craters begin to smooth over and the smoothing continues throughout the soaking period.

Pinholes smooth over more easily in fluid glazes and care should be taken to see that newly glazed pots are properly dried before the firing gathers speed.

Matt Glazes Turning Glossy

A matt glaze is essentially one that has a crystal structure; therefore it cannot be quite transparent. The development of crystals is achieved by having a high proportion of alumina, alkaline earth, or zinc in the mixture or another agent, such as rutile, which readily forms crystals on cooling. If such glazes are overfired, the matting agent is liable to be dissolved in the fluxes with the result that the glaze cools with a gloss. Slow cooling is essential to allow crystal formation.

Matting agents are more likely to be dissolved if they are ground excessively fine, because a greater surface area is then open to attack by the fluxes. Materials supplied by a reputable firm should not normally suffer from this defect and additional ball-milling or grinding is not advised.

Flow is not a property to be expected from matt glazes so the coating must be faultlessly applied and generally rather thicker than that of shiny glazes if the full qualities of the surface are to be brought out.

Underfiring and Overfiring

Glossy glazes which are underfired will also appear matt and slightly opaque, but the quality is not pleasant. It is also dangerous, because a glaze in this condition is open to chemical attack from acid foodstuffs. Such pots are easily refired.

Plate 24. *(Left) The white opaque earthenware pictured here has been deliberately overfired to reveal the indented clay texture. Photo: author.*

Plate 25. *(Above) This dark matt stoneware glaze has settled over a slight relief decoration. Denby Ware (England), Chevron pattern. Photo: author.*

Overfiring cannot be corrected, but when it happens by accident it sometimes reveals exciting qualities which can be brought under control (Plate 24). Overfiring of stoneware is, of course, disastrous to the kiln. However, earthenware—fired even as high as stoneware—does not necessarily cause much damage although this is dependent upon the clay.

Glazes that are overfired acquire different colors and textures in which there is a predominance of reds and red-browns, combined with interesting mottled effects. These changes in color and texture are caused by the iron content of the clay breaking through to the glaze surface. Red clays, when they do not melt, change from the usual pink to a pleasant brown or coffee color fused almost to glass on rims and ridges.

Upon overfiring, opaque glazes do not survive as dense coatings and the opacity disappears first from rims, although these may be left with a transparent coating (Plate 25). Browning of the rim is a problem that frequently occurs in the use of opaque glazes on red claywares, and it is a symptom of slight overfiring. The only cures, if overfiring is considered offensive, are to lower the firing temperature or to decrease the proportion of the fluid fluxes.

Color photographs by the author

Color Plate 1. Simple Borax Glazes *by Jackie Marsh. Domestic borax is mixed with different clays and applied to pinched bowls by brush, using as little water as possible.*

Color Plate 2. Simple Lead Glazes *by first-year students at the Bath Academy of Art, England. This earthenware is glazed with mixtures that are composed of lead bisilicate and clay. The mixtures, generally about 70% lead bisilicate to 30% clay, were arrived at by trial and error.*

Color Plate 3. Alkaline Turquoise Glaze. *This early example (about 1930) of studio pottery is covered with an alkaline glaze that contains copper oxide. A glaze of this type follows an ancient Middle Eastern tradition.*

Color Plate 4. American Lead-Glazed Slipware Dish. *Courtesy American Museum, Bath, England. Here is an example of trailed slipware with a lead glaze. Ware of this kind has been made all over Europe since the 16th century.*

Color Plate 5. Porcelain with Celadon Glaze *by W. Ruscoe. This hard-fired porcelain has a transparent celadon glaze over delicately incised lines. Such glazes date back to 10th century China.*

Color Plate 6. Italian Majolica. *Genoa, seventeenth century. Collection of the author. This finely painted dish is representative of the tin-glazed earthenware which has abounded in the Middle East and Europe since the 9th century.*

Color Plate 7. Salt-Glazed Ware *by Peter Hunt, Roger Holly, and David Pole. All these pots are finished with a salt glaze.*

Color Plate 8. Slate Glaze on Stoneware *by Kathleen Glaister. The rich iron glaze on this bowl is derived from the slates of the English Lake District.*

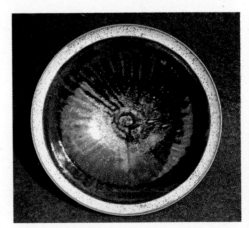

Color Plate 9. Stoneware Bowl *by David Green. On this bowl, a stoneware matt glaze is applied over a glossy iron one.*

Color Plate 10. Detail of a Stoneware Glaze *by Bryan Newman. Here an iron glaze is applied over slightly textured clay.*

Color Plate 11. Detail of a Stoneware Glaze *by Bryan Newman. Here a dense glaze is thickly applied over an iron glaze.*

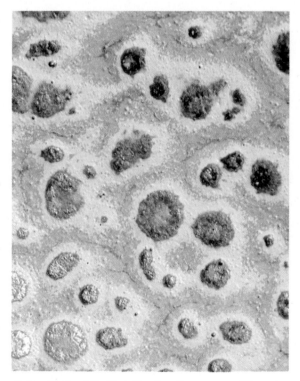

Color Plate 12. Detail of a Stoneware Glaze *by David Green. This matt glaze contains both vanadium and nickel.*

Color Plate 13. Detail of a Stoneware Glaze *by David Green. Mixed rocks and sea shells (which yield calcium) are used to produce this glaze.*

Color Plate 14. Effect of Pigment in Glaze. *Tests by Stephen Wharton. The glaze used here is given on page 49. Starting top row center, reading across, the glazes contain 2% iron, 2% manganese, 2% tin, 2% copper, and 2% cobalt respectively. The plain glaze is seen top row far left.*

Color Plate 15. Effect of Different Clays. *Tests by Colette Eade. Here the same stoneware glaze has been applied to five different clays.*

Color Plate 16. Effect of Various Firing Conditions *by Stephen Wharton. An iron glaze is applied in different thicknesses and fired in different situations in a kiln. The best results are obtained with fairly thin coats.*

Color Plate 17. Effect of Changes in Basic Constitution *by Joan Norman. The seven glazes seen here are made from mixtures of equal parts of pine ash together with one of the following: red clay, ball clay, china clay, yellow ochre (the darkest), Cornish stone, felspar, and flint.*

Color Plate 18. Ash-Glaze Painting *by Sally Higgins. Glazes, compounded from ashes, rocks, and earths, are used like watercolor to produce this landscape. The materials came directly from the countryside depicted in the painting. The painting was done on the spot.*

CHAPTER SEVEN

Coloring Glazes

The potter has at his disposal a range of color qualities and surface textures derived from the three-dimensional dispersion of coloring agents within the glaze coating (Plates 26 and 27). These qualities are all too often abandoned in insensitive attempts to imitate the high-pitched values of cellulose lacquer or glossy oil paint. The unique characteristics of ceramic pigmentation are the result of the reflection and absorption of parts of the spectrum of light from crystalline, colloidal, or minute individual particles within the glaze thickness.

The effects obtainable are capable of limitless manipulation because they are responsive to the chemistry of the glaze as well as to the strength with which the substances have been added, singly or in combination. The kind of clay underneath the glaze and the manner of firing also have an important bearing on the color and surface texture of the finished product (Color Plates 15 and 16, pages 94–95).

Pigments from Elements

Most of the elements used for making colors are next to one another in the Periodic Table (Table C, page 116) in situations where the inner shells of electrons are incomplete. It is evident that color formation is due in some circumstances to alterations of the position of electrons within the shells caused by the energy of light. In other cases, particularly in opaque glazes, the color is due to the simple refraction of the whole or parts of the light spectrum from the faces of complicated crystal structures lying within the glaze (Plate 26).

Most of the elements have by now been partially tested for their color reaction in ceramics, but the traditional range of pigments—antimony, cobalt, copper, chromium, iron, manganese and nickel with tin and titanium along with zirconium as opacifiers—has not been greatly extended for ordinary use. However, cadmium, selenium, praseodymium, wolfram, uranium, and vanadium have proved useful for certain purposes. The precious metals—gold, silver, and platinum—are used in low-temperature enamel decoration.

The pigments are procured from minerals known to us, in some cases, for many centuries. However, unlike the glaze ingredients their extraction and preparation into

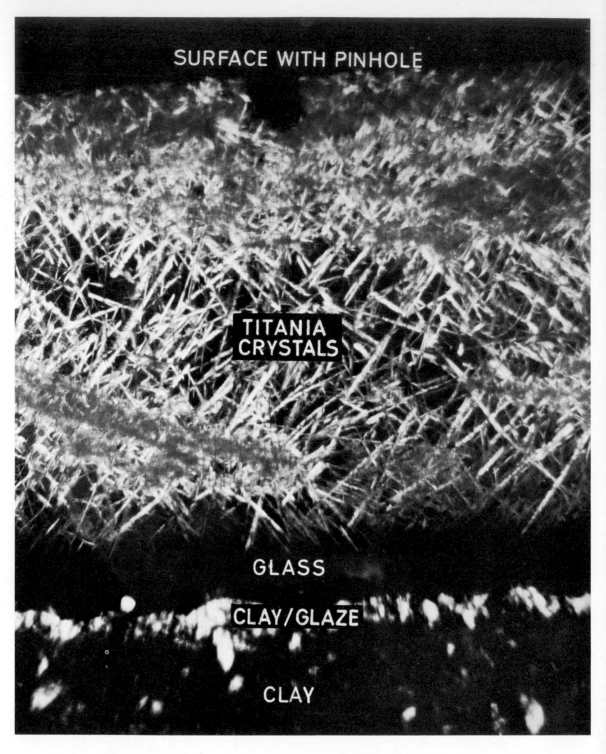

Plate 26. *Here is a section of a commercial matt opaque earthenware glaze magnified x 240. The matting and opacifying agent is rutile (crude ore of titanium oxide containing iron) and its effect is obtained by the mass of spiky titania crystals formed within the glass. A layer of clear glass is visible below the crystals and below that are some smaller crystals of sodium and calcium felspar at the point of interaction between glaze and body. Photo: British Ceramic Reserach Association.*

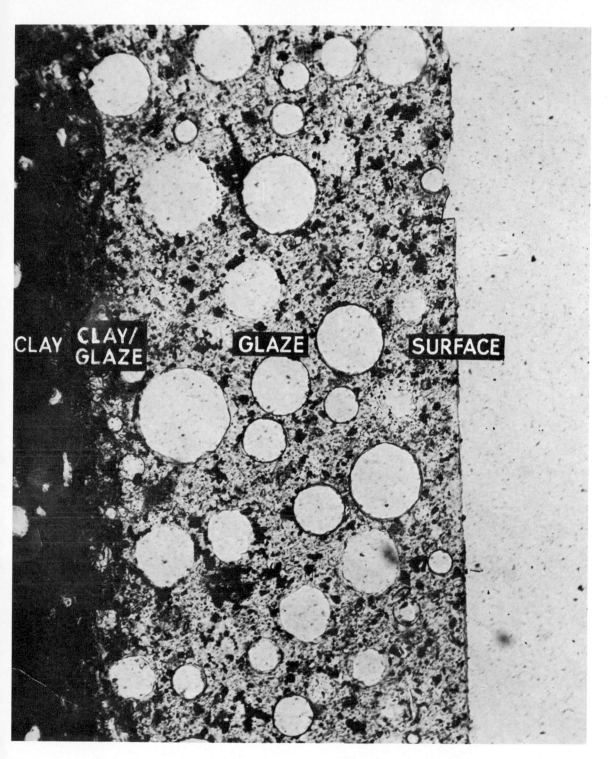

Plate 27. *This section of a semi-transparent, reduced stoneware glaze has been magnified x 144. The greater amalgamation of glaze and body caused by the high temperature is clearly seen when this photograph is compared with the previous earthenware example. The glaze is semi-transparent and glossy, and therefore, it contains few large crystals. The bubbles give it the pleasing quality of depth. The recipe for this glaze is found on page 49. It has been colored turquoise by the addition of 2% tin oxide, 1% chrome oxide, and ½% cobalt oxide. The black specks are probably caused by the chrome oxide. Photo: British Ceramic Research Association.*

suitable forms for use as glaze stains, underglaze colors, or on-glaze enamels involves elaborate chemical as well as physical procedures; therefore their prices are noticeably higher. In recent years both prices and availability have been affected by political situations in Africa and other places. For instance, uranium was unobtainable for many years, but it has come back now in the form of "spent" oxide from atomic energy undertakings.

Effects of Pigments on Behavior of Glazes

The pigments—usually in the form of metal oxides—are added to glazes singly or in combination in quite small amounts, rarely exceeding 10% of the total glaze batch. With small amounts the effect on the behavior of the glaze itself frequently is not noticed. However, larger additions—usually of oxides which make glazes white and opaque—can materially alter the fusibility of a glaze, so that an adjustment of the composition of the glaze becomes necessary. In this respect, the way in which reactions will occur can be predicted from the chemical formula of the oxide concerned. For instance, an oxide in which one atom of the metal is combined with two of oxygen will respond like silica, reducing fusibility; whereas an oxide in which the metal and oxygen are in equal ratio will behave as a flux.

Some potters include pigments in their glaze formula, and when this is done, any alteration to the fusibility can be compensated before the recipe is worked out. For example, an inclusion of a fluxing pigment (one in which only a single atom of oxygen is included in the formula) in the ratio of 0.1 molecules reduces the remainder of the fluxes to 0.9 when the formula is unified.

A List of Ceramic Pigments

The full subject of pigments and the formation of colors within glazes and bodies is extremely complicated and the following brief notes can only be considered as an introduction. It is advisable to keep careful records attached to your samples. Reference is made to the categories described in Chapter 4, Table 7. See also Table M, page 126, for formulas.

Antimony. 3% to 8%. Produces stable yellows in glazes of Category 1. Many potters prefer to use the lead antimonate in additions of up to 20%, because the raw oxide may cause blisters.

Chromium. 1% to 5%. Produces dark greens in most glazes (Category 3 or 11 recommended). In Category 1 red glazes are produced when alumina and silica are at their lowest (low-temperature earthenware only and *not* for food vessels). Pink is created when very small amounts of chromium are used in conjunction with tin (molecular ratio about $0.05\ Cr_2O_3$ to $0.1\ SnO_2$). Chromium colors are usually spoiled by zinc.

Cobalt. ¼% to 1%, sometimes up to 5%. A strong blue pigment is produced. Recommended for Categories 5 and 6 or 10 with magnesium also present.

Copper. 1% to 6%. Greens are created in most glazes. Turquoises are produced in Categories 5, 6 (Color Plate 3, page 90), 7, 10, and 12. Red is achieved with difficulty in Categories 8 and 11 in high-temperature reduced firings.

Iron. 1% to 12% or 14%. Extraordinary range of color and effects according to conditions. Black appears with high iron content, high silica, high temperature, and Category 9 glazes. Brown is produced from medium additions to most glazes (Categories 1 and 11 recommended). For greens, Category 11 is recommended (Color Plate 5, page 91) while reds are obtained from Category 9 with low alumina, and blue from Category 12 (barium) with small inclusions of boric oxide (see also Plates 28 and 29).

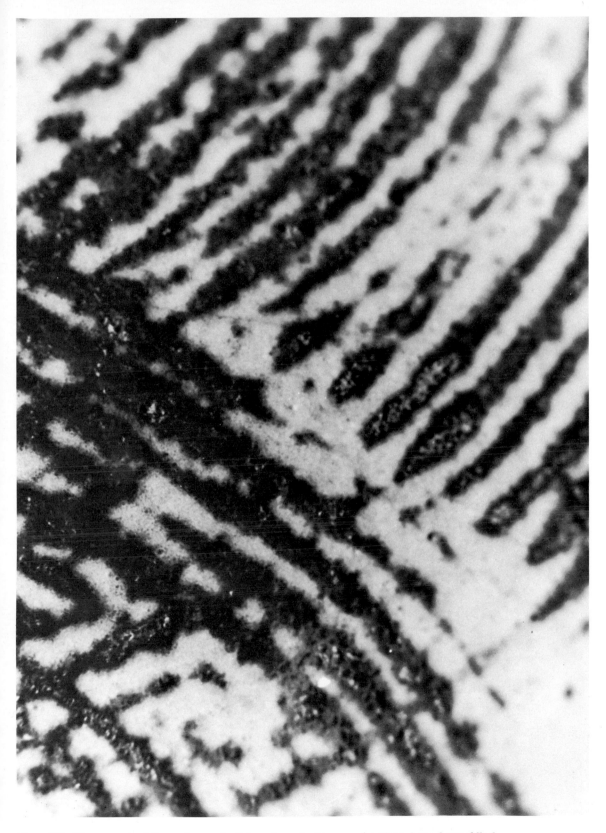

Plate 28. *The scratched lines shown in this enlarged closeup of a glaze have been filled, before biscuiting, with iron oxide. A matt stoneware glaze lies on top. Photo: author.*

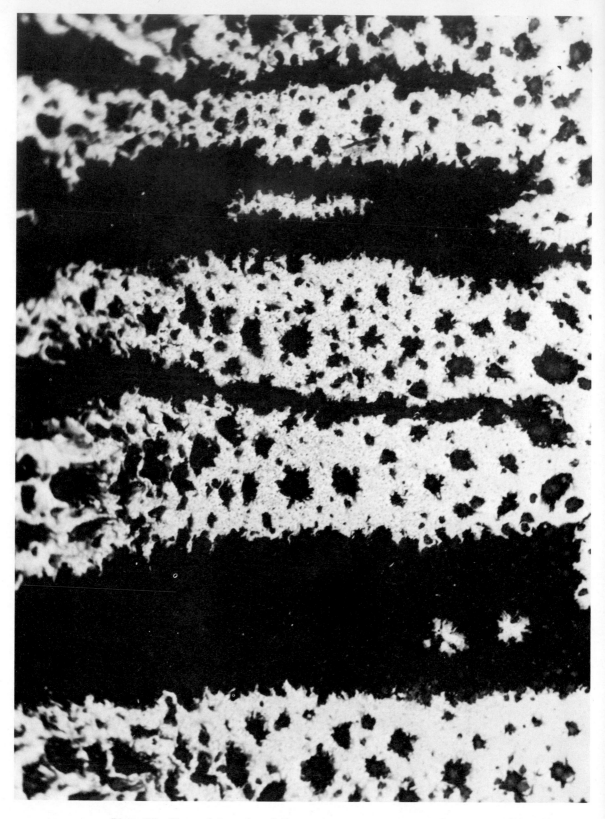

Plate 29. *Pictured here is a fully opaque, matt stoneware glaze over a glossy black iron glaze. This is a detail from a pattern made by using wax resist between the two glazes. Photo: author.*

Manganese. 2% to 10%. Purple-brown is produced in Category 1 glazes, while claret-brown is created in Category 2, and purple and violet in Category 6.

Nickel. 1% to 4%. Generally grayed colors. For greens, Categories 2 and 4 recommended, and for blue, Category 1 with zinc and low alumina.

Uranium. 5% to 10%. Red is created with Category 1 glazes with low temperature and no calcium, borax, or much alkali. Yellow is created with Category 3 glazes.

Vanadium. 5% to 10%. Produces yellows at high-temperature. Usually added as vanadium stain at up to 10%.

Opacifiers

The three chief opacifiers are less affected by the composition of the glaze than many of the coloring oxides, and are generally used in larger amounts. Any of the pigments just listed can be used in conjunction with opacifiers to give colored opaque glazes.

Tin. 8% to 10%. Tin oxide is the favorite opacifier but its price is becoming prohibitive in some circumstances (Color Plate 6, page 91).

Titanium. 5% to 15%. Titanium oxide can considerably alter the colors of other oxides painted on top of it, or used in with the glaze, and sometimes produces crystalline effects. The crude ore, rutile, which is a mixture of titanium and iron oxides, is favored for the production of mottled glazes (Plate 26). Titanium in amounts less than 5% can produce pleasing blue colors at high temperatures. Combinations of tin and titanium are effective.

Zirconium. 10% to 20%. This is cheapest of the opacifiers and the least effective; 20% of zirconium may be required to produce an opacity similar to that produced with 10% of tin and the result will be decidedly creamy. Zircon is a chemical combination of zirconium and silica ($ZnSiO_4$) and an inclusion of 20% would usually necessitate some alteration of the glaze formula.

Kiln Atmospheres

Changes of atmosphere inside the kiln can alter some of the colors just described. Most kilns that fire efficiently have an atmosphere inside which contains plenty of oxygen. This is certainly true of all electric kilns, because no fuel is burned in them to produce heat. However, the extraction of heat from any other fuels—such as gas or coal—can only be achieved by supplying adequate quantities of oxygen to combine with (or burn) the carbon and hydrogen that these fuels contain. If too little oxygen is available to complete the burning of all the fuel, then the hot carbon in the kiln interior will attack the pots themselves in an attempt to extract the oxygen from the oxides that make up the pots' composition.

The ability to withstand such attack from the two most oxygen-hungry elements of all—carbon and hydrogen—demonstrates again the stability of ceramic products which makes them indispensable wherever resistance to weather, extreme heat, or strong chemical attack is required. Remember that the attack of the reducing gases takes place at a critical moment when the oxides are red hot and their electrons are moving outwards from one level to another, further away from the attractive forces of their own nuclei and into positions which strain to the utmost the efficiency of any bonding arrangement.

Reduced Firing and Pottery Goods

Some of the oxides used for coloring glazes—especially iron and copper—and one of the fluxes—lead—are unable to withstand the attack. It is interesting to note the relative positions of these metals in the Periodic Table (Table C, page 116). These are the easiest metals to obtain from their ores and, therefore, among the first to be used by mankind. Reference has already been made to the difficulty and cost of separating aluminum from oxygen.

Copper is only present in measurable and effective quantities in pottery goods when it has been deliberately added. Iron, as we have seen before, is always present from trace to 8% or 10%, and it is not surprising that a reducing atmosphere, or one that is short of oxygen, should have a considerable effect. Iron is present in clays as well as glazes, and many of the pleasanter qualities derived from a reduction firing are due to this fact (Color Plate 15, page 94) although if too much iron is present—as in a red clay—the result is likely to be disastrous. The resulting color varies, but recognized stoneware clays usually turn out a warm ochre or orange. The process is sometimes used in industry on white clays or porcelain bodies, during the biscuit firing, in order to change the slightly cream color to a blue-gray that looks whiter than it is.

The warmed color of reduced clay is not the result of reduction itself, but of reoxidation of the surface during the cooling of the kiln. When the clay surface has been sealed by a fused glaze, the gray color of reduced clay is retained, exerting considerable effect on the color of the glaze. If a reducing atmosphere is not present until after a glaze has begun to fuse, the clay will not be altered and the result may be disappointing. If too much reduction smoke is introduced at the time the glaze is fusing, carbon may become entrapped in the glass giving a decidedly dead quality to the finished product.

The quality of reduction firing is most easily judged on items coated with transparent, colorless glazes and one or two examples of this kind should be included in different parts of the kiln as tests. Trapped carbon, areas of reoxidation, and others of sealed reduction, can sometimes be clearly distinguished across the thickness of the clay when finished specimens are broken. The speckled "bird's egg" quality of reduced glazes is due entirely to the effect of reduction on particles of iron minerals in the clay, and it cannot be induced by addition to the glaze.

Reduction Firing with Iron and Copper

Most glazes used in reduction fires are pigmented with iron and in them, too, one of the attractive features is the reoxidizing of the iron in the thinner parts of the glaze during the cooling of the kiln. This causes brilliant red flashes around the rims or the ridges that were produced by the thrower's finger (Color Plates 10 and 11, page 93). The red color comes from the commonest and most stable oxide of the metal, ferric oxide (Fe_2O_3). The other colors are caused by the reduced variety, ferrous oxide (FeO), and at times particles of the pure metal stripped of all oxygen embedded in the glaze. The colors possible range from the lovely celadon greens to blues, grays, and black, according to the amount of iron present and, as with the other coloring oxides, according to the fluxes present in the glaze mixture.

Copper behaves similarly in reduction fires; the usual green effects obtained with cupric oxide (CuO) are converted to a variety of reds formed from cuprous oxide (Cu_2O) or again the bare metal. These changes are often highly prized and they are generally more difficult to obtain than any from iron. It is often necessary to maintain the reduction during cooling to preserve them.

Reduction Firing and Lead

The effect of reducing lead oxide is disastrous, because the glaze mixture itself is deprived of some necessary oxygen, but the red colors of reduced copper can be achieved in low earthenware glazes (Category 2 with some tin) by keeping the reduction light from 900°C. (1652°F.) onwards, alternating it with frequent periods of oxidation, and contin-

Plate 30. *The decoration on this plate is painted in lustre over an opacified glaze. This plate is a rich example of the Moorish pottery described on page 106. Photo: G.H.W. Sheard.*

uing reduction during cooling from 700°C. (1292°F.) downwards. The final maturing of the glaze should be effected under oxidizing conditions.

Achieving Reduction

There is no great mystery or special difficulty about achieving reduction, although the control of special colors may not be easy. In most kilns a surplus of fuel, or shortage of oxygen to consume it, can be arranged by slowly closing air vents until a flickering yellow flame is produced. If the ware is shut away from the flames completely, as in a muffle kiln, it may be necessary to introduce carbon into the interior of the muffle. This can be done by pushing small pieces of wood or other carbon products through the spy-hole. (Mothballs were used at one time as a convenient source of pure carbon, but they are no longer composed of this element). Because the process is, in reality, one of inefficient fuel consumption, it is not advisable or necessary to proceed in this way throughout the entire firing. The process should start, however, before the glaze begins to melt in order to change the clay beneath.

For most stoneware, 1100°C. (2012°F.) is a reasonable starting point. To obtain pleasing red, the process should be stopped at about 1230°C. (2246°F.) and the last 50°C. (122°F.) or 70°C. (152°F.) of the firing, as well as the first 100°C. (212°F.) or so of cooling, carried on with ample air supply.

It is not advisable to try reduction in electric kilns. Although the elements may not appear to be much affected (they are said to be coated with alumina after the first firing), the process "sweats out" and reduces minute particles of iron-laden clays or other glaze ingredients embedded in the channels and refractories of even the best-kept kilns. The reduced particles then cause the elements to fuse and break.

Reduced Stoneware and Porcelain

Stoneware firings without reduction are often referred to as "oxidized" but this is misleading because, in fact, no such chemical change takes place. The oxides in such a firing merely remain as they are.

The special beauties of reduced stoneware and porcelain glazes were first understood and brought under control by the Chinese; the wares they produced are mostly of this kind. The process is generally associated with high-temperature wares, and it was avoided in Europe and the Middle East because of the prevalence of lead-glazed earthenware. The Moorish potters did, however, succeed in producing a special kind of reduced earthenware known as *lustre* (Plate 30) which can be very pleasing. This was produced over a glaze, high in potassium and soda, to which copper or silver sulphides were applied as pastes and fired, like enamels, in a second firing. The reduction took place between 700°C. (1292°F.) and 800°C. (1472°F.) during this second firing, and the kiln was shut off before the glaze itself began to melt.

CHAPTER EIGHT

Using a Slide Rule

It is no exaggeration to say that a slide rule reduces the work of hours to a matter of minutes, and—although the instruments may look formidable to the uninitiated—there are no difficulties in their use which cannot be overcome by a few minutes of practice. Most of the available models have four or more lines of scales fulfilling a variety of mathematical functions, but for your purpose only those lettered C and D are required. For maximum accuracy and easy use, the scales should be no less than 10" long and clearly engraved on the matt surface of a solid plastic body. Some suppliers of slide rules are listed on page 142.

The theory behind a slide rule can be demonstrated by the use of two ordinary rulers in the following way (see Figure 12). If 0 on the top ruler is set opposite 2 on the bottom one, the sum of 2 plus any figure along the top is found opposite to it on the bottom scale.

Similarly the result of the subtraction of the figures on the top from those opposite to them on the bottom is found on the bottom ruler, opposite 0 on the top. In Figure 12 the answer is, of course, always 2.

Although no one would bother with an instrument only capable of solving such elementary problems, it is this principle of addition and subtraction by two rulers which is used on a slide rule. The difference is that the scales on a slide rule are subdivided in logarithmic progression rather than equally. Logarithms are added for multiplication and subtracted for division; so the result of setting the end of the top scale of a slide rule (marked 1 not 0) against 2 on the bottom scale is to multiply the figures along the top by 2 (see Figure 13). Note: If the previous method of subtraction shown in Figure 13 is carried out, the result is a division; 6 on the bottom is opposite 3 on the top, and the answer for 6 ÷ 3 is on the bottom scale opposite the end of the top 1.

Using the letter C to represent the sliding scale (top) and D for the fixed one (bottom), and using also the moveable hairline, or cursor (which comes with a slide rule to assist your reading from one scale to another), the procedure for multiplying and dividing on a slide rule can be summarized as follows.

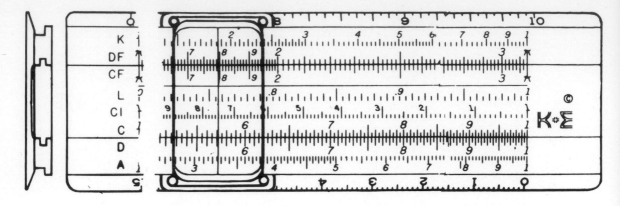

Plate 31. *This modern polyphase slide rule (model 68-1576) is manufactured by Keuffel & Esser and is available in most art supply stores for under $15.00. It has a plastic, 10" unbreakable indicator. Courtesy Keuffel & Esser, Inc.*

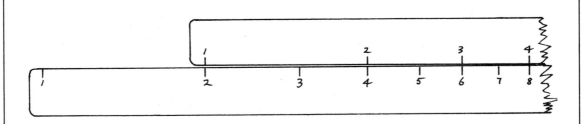

Figure 12. *The principle upon which the slide rule operates is illustrated by using two ordinary rulers placed one on top of another (see page 107).*

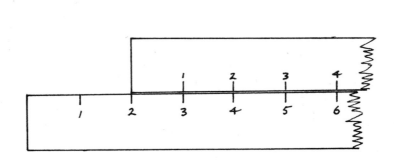

Figure 13. *The slide rule has a top scale that begins with 1, not 0 as in our example shown in Figure 12. By setting the top scale against two on the lower one, all the figures along the top scale are multiplied by two and the results are shown on the bottom scale directly beneath the figures on the top scale.*

Multiplying with a Slide Rule

x x y

Step 1. Opposite x on the scale D, set 1 or 10 on scale C.

Step 2. Set cursor over y on scale C.

Step 3. The answer is found under the hairline on D.

Dividing with a Slide Rule

$x \div y$ or $\dfrac{x}{y}$

Step 1. Set cursor over x on scale D.

Step 2. Slide y on C under the hairline.

Step 3. The answer is found on D opposite 1 or 10 on C.

In multiplication, it matters little which figure is multiplied by which, but the order obviously does matter in the case of division; $4 \div 2$ is not the same as $2 \div 4$! A simple rule for remembering the position of the figures on the scales of a slide rule when dividing is that they should be reversed. Instead of x/y, x is found on the bottom scale (D) and y on the top (C).

Reading the Scales

The position of decimal points is ignored while setting figures on a slide rule; decimals are inserted in relevant positions in the answer afterwards. For example, 400, 40, 4, 0.4 and 0.04 are all set at the point marked 4 and 3250, 325, 32.5, 3.25 or even 0.0325 are all set at 325 as shown in Figure 14. (At 314, π is usually indicated for the convenience of calculation involving circles.) For example, if you multiply 0.4 by 3.25, the slide rule provides an answer of 13 which, when the decimal point is inserted, becomes 1.3.

For the same reason, either 1 at the left-hand end or 10 at the right may be used in calculations according to which is convenient for the situation of the other figures involved.

The single digit numbers are set on the chief divisions shown on the rule. The second digit of a two or three digit number is set at one of the nine subdivisions between the main divisions. Any third digit is set at one of the smallest divisions, of which there are more at the left of the rule than the right because of the greater spaces between them. Fourth figures can only be set approximately along much of a ten-inch slide rule, but this degree of accuracy is adequate for all ordinary uses. Cylindrical rulers, where the spirally engraved scale can measure 60 or more inches in length, provide accurate settings to five or six digits.

Common misreadings occur at points between 1 (10) and 11, 2 (20) and 21, 3 (30) and 31 etc. The point marked A in Figure 15 could be misread as 22, whereas it is in fact 202. Similarly 1905 can be misread as 195.

Positioning the Decimal Point

There are rules for determining the position of decimal points in the answers to slide rule calculation, as indeed there are for long multiplication or division. However, many people favor the use of approximate calculations which also provide a guard against misreadings. The majority of cases present no problems, but there are some, especially where one or more numbers are less than one, which may appear awkward. Here again a "reversal" rule

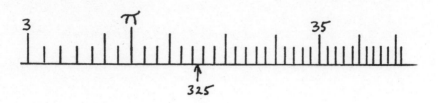

Figure 14. *The position of decimal points is ignored while setting figures on a slide rule. As seen here 3250, 325, 3.25, 0.0325 are all set at 325 on the rule.*

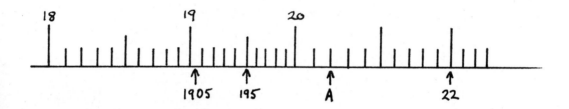

Figure 15. *Seen here is an example of a common misreading of a slide rule. Point A could be misread as 22 when, in fact, it is 202.*

aids the memory: *multiplication by a figure less than 1 results in a decrease, whereas dividing by less than 1 results in an increase.*

This comes about in the following way. Multiplying by a half is the same as saying "half of" whereas in dividing by a half the answer is double the original figure because there are twice as many halves.

In the example shown in Figure 14, 0.4 x 3.25, 0.4 is a little less than half so that the answer could be expected to be somewhere around 1.4. The slide rule showed 13, therefore the correct answer with the decimal point inserted is 1.3.

Examples Using the Glaze Calculations from Chapter 3

Slide rules are hardly necessary in converting from a formula to a recipe using the theoretical composition of minerals. The example 0.4 x 3.25 could be done by thinking of 0.4 as 4/10, in which case the answer is found by multiplying by 4 and dividing by 10 by moving the decimal point one place to the left. This method would serve for all the multiplications at the conclusion of Step 5 in the "Formula to Recipe" section of Chapter 3 (0.3 = 3/10, 0.2 = 1/5) except for flint which is a simple multiplication problem.

In the next glaze calculation in Chapter 3—converting a recipe to its formula—division is involved. Approximate calculations could be carried out by the standard trial and error method as follows:

Step 1. Felspar 26.7 ÷ 556.8 (approximately 550).

Step 2. 550 into 26 does not go, so the answer will be 0.???

Step 3. 550 into 260 does not go, so the answer will be 0.0??

Step 4. 550 into 2600 does go, just under 5 times, so the answer will be 0.04?

The ?? are now filled in by a reading from the slide rule which also confirms the estimated 4. The answer is 0.048.

For dolomite 184.4 is approximated to 200, china clay to 250, and flint to 60. Whiting only involves moving the decimal two places to the left as the 0.1 is too small to be effective.

Calculating Percentages and Unifying

A great deal of time can be saved in these tedious operations which involve dividing a number of figures by their total, in order to express them as parts per 100, or as a fraction of 1. Each division can be done separately according to the method already described. However, as the divisor is the same in all cases, the process could obviously be speeded up by setting the divisor on the fixed scale, D, with the cursor and finding the answers on scale C opposite 1 or 10 on D. The procedure follows:

Step 1. Add the figures together and set cursor over the total on fixed scale D.

Step 2. Move the slide (scale C) until the first of the figures to be reduced is under the hairline.

Step 3. The answer is found on C opposite 1 or 10 on D. Steps 2 and 3 are repeated for each figure.

Assessment of the position of the decimal point can again be made by approximate calculations. In the case of percentages, the size of the sum provides a ready guide to the position of the decimal point. If the figures (for example, page 51) add up to 417.6 then each figure will yield about one-fourth of its original amount when expressed as a percentage. Division by 4 would, therefore, show the number of figures to be expected before and after the decimal point.

In unifying, the sum of the fluxes usually adds up to a figure less than 1 and, therefore, division of each by this total results in an increase. In the calculation involving unifying, the sum is 0.239 (about one-fourth) so that multiplication by 4 gives an indication of the number of figures before and after the decimal point.

The result of both calculations should always be checked by addition, percentages adding, of course, to within a decimal place or two of 100 and the results of unifying to within a point or two of 1.

Tables

°C.	°F.	°C.	°F.	°C.	°F.	°C.	°F.
100	212	500	932	900	1652	1300	2372
110	230	510	950	910	1670	1320	2408
120	248	520	968	920	1688	1340	2444
130	266	530	986	930	1706	1360	2480
140	284	540	1004	940	1724	1380	2516
150	302	550	1022	950	1742	1400	2552
160	320	560	1044	960	1760	1420	2588
170	338	570	1058	970	1778	1440	2624
180	356	580	1076	980	1796	1460	2660
190	374	590	1094	990	1814	1480	2696
200	392	600	1112	1000	1832	1500	2732
210	410	610	1130	1010	1850	1520	2768
220	428	620	1148	1020	1868	1540	2804
230	446	630	1166	1030	1886	1560	2840
240	464	640	1184	1040	1904	1580	2876
250	482	650	1202	1050	1922	1600	2912
260	500	660	1220	1060	1940	1620	2948
270	518	670	1238	1070	1958	1640	2984
280	536	680	1256	1080	1976	1660	3020
290	554	690	1274	1090	1994	1680	3056
300	572	700	1292	1100	2012	1700	3092
310	590	710	1310	1110	2030	1720	3128
320	608	720	1328	1120	2048	1740	3164
330	626	730	1346	1130	2066	1760	3200
340	644	740	1364	1140	2084	1780	3236
350	662	750	1382	1150	2102	1800	3272
360	680	760	1400	1160	2120	1820	3308
370	698	770	1418	1170	2138	1840	3344
380	716	780	1436	1180	2156	1860	3380
390	734	790	1454	1190	2174	1880	3416
400	752	800	1472	1200	2192	1900	3452
410	770	810	1490	1210	2210	1920	3488
420	788	820	1508	1220	2228	1940	3524
430	806	830	1526	1230	2246	1960	3560
440	824	840	1544	1240	2264	1980	3596
450	842	850	1562	1250	2282	2000	3632
460	860	860	1580	1260	2300	2100	3812
470	878	870	1598	1270	2318	2200	3992
480	896	880	1616	1280	2336	2300	4172
490	914	890	1634	1290	2354	2400	4352

TABLE B. THE ELEMENTS USED IN CERAMICS

Element	Symbol	Atomic Wt. Approx. (C = 12)	Melting Point, °C.	Melting Point of Oxide, °C.
Aluminium	Al	27.0	660°	2050°
Antimony	Sb	121.8	630°	600°
Barium	Ba	137.3	704°	1923°
Bismuth	Bi	9.0	269°	820°–860°
Boron	B	10.8	2250°	577°
Cadmium	Cd	112.4	321°	900°
Calcium	Ca	40.1	852°	2570°
Carbon	C	12.0	volatilizes above 3000°	gas
Chlorine	Cl	35.5	−103°	gas
Chromium	Cr	52.0	1831°	2060°
Cobalt	Co	58.9	1492°	2860°
Copper	Cu	63.5	1084°	CuO 1148° and Cu$_2$O 1235°
Fluorine	F	19.0	−224°	gas
Gold	Au	197.0	1063°	dissociates on heating
Hydrogen	H	1.01	−257°	water
Iron	Fe	55.9	1526°	Fe$_2$O$_3$ 1565° and FeO 1420°
Lead	Pb	207.2	327°	880°
Lithium	Li	6.9	186°	618°
Magnesium	Mg	24.3	649°	2800°
Manganese	Mn	54.9	1242°	1650°
Nickel	Ni	58.7	1455°	2090°
Nitrogen	N	14.0	−210°	gas
Oxygen	O	16.0	−219°	−
Phosphorus	P	31.0	44°	vaporizes 250°–300°
Potassium	K	39.1	64°	red heat
Silicon	Si	28.1	1415°	1713°
Silver	Ag	107.9	960°	dissociates on heating
Sodium	Na	23.0	98°	red heat
Strontium	Sr	87.6	772°	2430°
Sulphur	S	32.1	116°	gas
Tin	Sn	118.7	232°	1127°
Titanium	Ti	47.9	1798°	1560°–1640°
Uranium	U	238.0	1132°	2176°
Vanadium	V	50.9	1900°	690°
Zinc	Zn	65.4	419°	1800°
Zirconium	Zr	91.2	1856°	2700°

TABLE C. PERIODIC TABLE OF THE ELEMENTS

NEW SHELLS
COMMENCING
TO FILL

THE LIGHT METALS

THE HEAVY MET

	L	3 LITHIUM Li	4 BERYL-LIUM Be						
	M	11 SODIUM Na	12 MAGNESIUM Mg						
	N	19 POTAS-SIUM K	20 CALCIUM Ca	21 SCAN-DIUM Sc	22 TITA-NIUM Ti	23 VANA-DIUM V	24 CHRO-MIUM Cr	25 MANGA-NESE Mn	26 IRON Fe
	O	37 RUBID-IUM Rb	38 STRON-TIUM Sr	39 YTTRI-UM Y	40 ZIRCO-NIUM Zr	41 NIOBIUM Nb	42 MOLYB-DENUM Mo	43 TECH-NETIUM Tc	44 RUTH-NIUM Ru
	P	55 CAESIUM Cs	56 BARIUM Ba	57 LANTHA-NUM La	72 HAF-NIUM Hf	73 TANTA-LUM Ta	74 WOLFRAM W	75 RHENIUM Re	76 OSMIU Os
	Q	87 FRAN-CIUM Fr	88 RADIUM Ra	89 ACTINI-UM Ac	90 THORIUM Th	91 PROTO-ACTINIUM Pa	92 URANIUM U		

58-71 THE RARE

90-103 THE ACTI

GROUP NUMBERS	1A	2A	3A	4A	5A	6A	7A

THE ALKALIES

THE ALKALINE EARTHS

CERAMIC FUNCTIONS	FLUXES OR NETWORK MODIFIERS	OPACIFIERS. PIGMENTS. LIGHT ———————

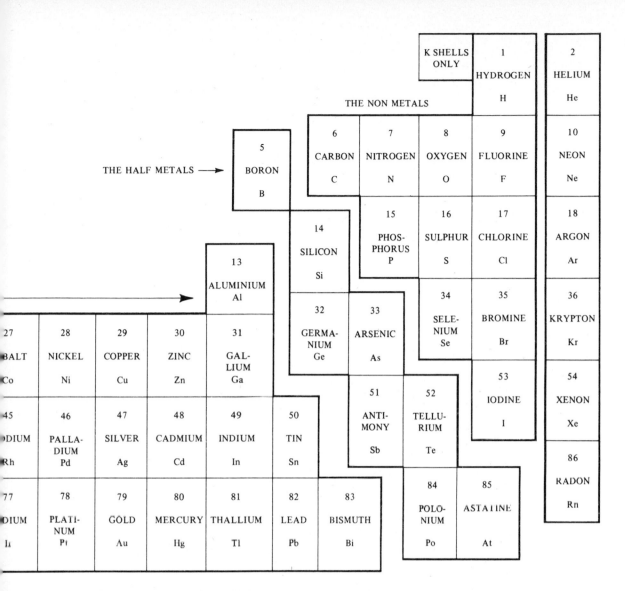

				K SHELLS ONLY	1 HYDROGEN H	2 HELIUM He
			THE NON METALS			
		5 BORON B	6 CARBON C	7 NITROGEN N	8 OXYGEN O	9 FLUORINE F	10 NEON Ne

THE HALF METALS →

| | | | | 13
ALUMINIUM
Al | 14
SILICON
Si | 15
PHOS-PHORUS
P | 16
SULPHUR
S | 17
CHLORINE
Cl | 18
ARGON
Ar |

| 27
BALT
Co | 28
NICKEL
Ni | 29
COPPER
Cu | 30
ZINC
Zn | 31
GAL-LIUM
Ga | 32
GERMA-NIUM
Ge | 33
ARSENIC
As | 34
SELE-NIUM
Se | 35
BROMINE
Br | 36
KRYPTON
Kr |

| 45
DIUM
Rh | 46
PALLA-DIUM
Pd | 47
SILVER
Ag | 48
CADMIUM
Cd | 49
INDIUM
In | 50
TIN
Sn | 51
ANTI-MONY
Sb | 52
TELLU-RIUM
Te | 53
IODINE
I | 54
XENON
Xe |

| 77
DIUM
Ir | 78
PLATI-NUM
Pt | 79
GOLD
Au | 80
MERCURY
Hg | 81
THALLIUM
Tl | 82
LEAD
Pb | 83
BISMUTH
Bi | 84
POLO-NIUM
Po | 85
ASTATINE
At | 86
RADON
Rn |

– CERIUM, PRASEODYMIUM, NDOEYMIUM, PROMETHIUM, SAMARIUM, EUROPIUM, GADOLINIUM, TERBIUM, DYSPROSI-UM HOLMIUM, ERBIUM, THULIUM, YTTERBIUM, LUTECIUM.

TALS – NEPTUNIUM, PLOTUNIUM, AMERICIUM, CURIUM, BERKELIUM, CALIFORNIUM, EINSTEINIUM, FERMIUM, MEN-DELEVIUM, NOBELIUM.

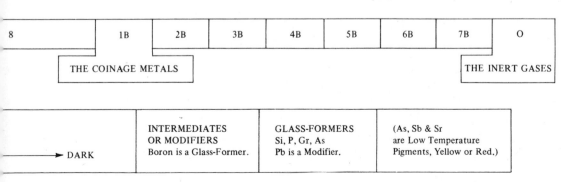

| 8 | 1B | 2B | 3B | 4B | 5B | 6B | 7B | O |

THE COINAGE METALS   THE INERT GASES

| → DARK | INTERMEDIATES OR MODIFIERS
Boron is a Glass-Former. | GLASS-FORMERS
Si, P, Gr, As
Pb is a Modifier. | (As, Sb & Sr are Low Temperature Pigments, Yellow or Red.) |

Temperatures	Orton Cones (at 150°C. per hr.)	Staffordshire Cones	Flux	Usual Ranges of Molecular Proportions in Unified Formulas			
				Alumina	Silica	Boric Oxide in Lead Glazes	Boric Oxide in Leadless Glazes
880°C. 1616°F.	012 (875°C.) [1607°F.]	011	1	0.1–0.15	1.25–2.0	0.4–0.5	0.8–1.5
980°C. 1796°F.	07 (990°C.) [1814°F.]	06	1	0.15–0.25	1.5–2.5	0.3–0.5	0.6–1.0
1080°C. 1976°F.	04 (1060°C.) [1940°F.]	01	1	0.15–0.3	1.75–3.0	0.25–0.5	0.5–0.75
1180°C. 2156°F.	3 (1170°C.) [2138°F.]	5	1	0.2–0.35	2.5–3.5	0.25–0.4	0.3–0.5
1280°C. 2336°F.	9 (1285°C.) [2345°F.]	9	1	0.3–0.7	3.0–5.0	–	0.15–0.3

Notes: The temperatures and cone numbers are to be regarded as the centers of a range of between 20°C. and 40°C. on either side.

The limits shown represent a middle range of ratios and there are many published formulas containing more or less of either oxide. For possible subdividion of the unit of flux see Table E.

Effects of Boric Oxide: Reduces crazing, enhances brilliance, and increases elasticity.

Effect of Boric Oxide on Pigments: Assists iron blues (11), copper reds (11), copper turquoise (5 and 6), manganese purples (2) and quietens cobalt blues (5, 6 and 7). (Numbers refer to glaze categories, Table 7, page 57.)

TABLE E. USUAL RATIOS OF MOLECULES OF THE COMMON FLUXES IN UNIFIED GLAZE FORMULAS

Temperature and Type of Glaze		Calcium Oxide	Magnesium Oxide	Barium Oxide	The Alkalies	Lead Oxide	Zinc Oxide
880°C. [1616°F.]	Lead	0.1–0.2	0–0.05	0–0.05	0.15–0.3	0.5–0.85	0–0.05
	Leadless	0.15–0.5	0–0.1	0–0.1	0.35–0.5	–	0–0.05
980°C. [1796°F.]	Lead	0.15–0.325	0.05–0.15	0.075–0.15	0.15–0.3	0.4–0.8	0.075–0.15
	Leadless	0.25–0.5	0.075–0.15	0.1–0.2	0.35–0.5	–	0.05–0.1
1080°C. [1976°F.]	Lead	0.15–0.35	0.1–0.15	0.1–0.2	0.15–0.3	0.35–0.6	0.1–0.2
	Leadless	0.3–0.6	0.1–0.15	0.1–0.2	0.3–0.5	–	0.1–0.15
1180°C. [2156°F.]	Lead	0.25–0.45	0.1–0.15	0.1–0.2	0.2–0.35	0.25–0.55	0.15–0.2
	Leadless	0.3–0.6	0.1–0.2	0.1–0.3	0.2–0.5	–	0.1–0.25
1280°C. [2336°F.]	Leadless	0.35–0.7	0.1–0.35	0.1–0.3	0.2–0.5	–	0.15–0.35

Note: The limits shown represent a middle range of ratios, and there are many published formulas containing more or less of either oxide.

TABLE F. SOME CHARACTERISTICS OF BASIC FLUXES

Fluxes	Chief Insoluble Sources*	Effect of Small Inclusions	Effect of Large Inclusions	Effect on Pigments†
Calcium Oxide	Carbonates, silicate, and aluminium silicate.	Provides hardness and durability to lead and alkaline glazes. Decreases lead solubility.	In high temperature glazes produces glossy, durable finishes, but high amounts, together with low alumina/silica ratios produce matt qualities at all temperatures. Cheap and very useful.	Recommended for reds (11, reduced), celadons (11, reduced), chrome greens (3, 11), and uranium yellows (3).
Magnesium Oxide	Carbonates and silicate.	Improves glaze fit.	Induces mattness at all temperatures. Used especially to produce smooth, fatty, opaque matts at high temperatures.	Recommended for cobalt purples (7), cobalt pinks (12), and nickel greens (4). Not recommended for high temperature iron glazes or chrome reds (1).
Barium Oxide	Carbonate (all compounds poisonous).	Improves fusibility and gloss.	Mattness.	Heightens most colors. Especially recommended in celadons (11), but not iron reds (10) or chrome greens (1).
The Alkalies	Aluminium silicates only (lithium carbonate is insoluble).	Improve fusibility and can control peeling or flaking. Increase lead solubility.	Glossy and highly fusible glazes almost certainly crazed because of high shrinkage. The most reactive fluxes, easily obtained from common minerals, although always together with high proportions of alumina and silica.	Recommended for cobalt blues (5 and 6), copper turquoise (5 and 6), iron reds (10), chrome yellows (1), and manganese violets (6).
Lead Oxide	Lead silicates (oxides, carbonates and sulphide are insoluble but poisonous).	Increases fusibility.	Standard earthenware glossy and highly fusible glazes. Easily adjusted and applied – blemishes smooth over. Often used with boric oxide which improves craze resistance and stability against chemical attack.	Good with most pigments. Especially recommended for iron tan, browns or reds (1), uranium yellows (3), and reds (4).
Zinc Oxide	Oxide and carbonate.	Can bleach yellowness of lead glazes and improve resistance to crazing.	May cause blistering and problems in application, but can be controlled to provide matt or crystalline surfaces. The latter are especially sought for decorative purposes.	Recommended for nickel greens (4), uranium reds (4), and yellows (3). Not recommended with copper (6), iron, or chrome in any glazes.

*See Table M for details.

†Numbers in parentheses in the last column on the right refer to the glaze categories found in Table 7, page 57.

Clays	Loss %	Silica %	TiO$_2$ %	Alumina %	Fe$_2$O$_3$ %	Other Fluxes %	
Pure Clay substance	13.95	46.1	–	39.3	–	–	
China Clay (typical)	12.4	46.7	–	38.9	0.6	K$_2$O	0.96
						Na$_2$O	0.04
						MgO	0.02
						CaO	0.05
						total	1.07
Zettlitz Kaolin (as used by Seger)	12.86	46.82	–	38.49	1.09	K$_2$O	1.40
						Na$_2$O	–
						MgO	trace
						CaO	–
						total	1.40
Blue Ball Clay	9.35	50.5	0.91	33.55	1.48	K$_2$O	2.5
						Na$_2$O	0.3
						MgO	0.65
						CaO	0.26
						total	3.71
Stoneware Ball Clay	8.5	58.7	1.67	26.72	0.75	K$_2$O	2.66
						Na$_2$O	0.44
						MgO	0.41
						CaO	0.32
						total	3.83
Red Clay	7.12	59.6	1.28	21.94	6.56	K$_2$O	0.84
						Na$_2$O	0.82
						MgO	0.82
						CaO	0.59
						total	3.07
Aluminous Fireclay	14.1	43.4	3.35	36.89	0.69	K$_2$O	0.50
						Na$_2$O	0.26
						MgO	–
						CaO	0.78
						total	1.54
Siliceous Fireclay	7.31	68.7	1.22	18.67	2.37	K$_2$O	0.96
						Na$_2$O	0.08
						MgO	0.33
						CaO	0.23
						total	1.60

TABLE H. ACTUAL AND THEORETICAL PERCENTAGE COMPOSITIONS OF GLAZE INGREDIENTS

Glaze Ingredients	K_2O	Na_2O	CaO	MgO	Fe_2O_3	Al_2O_3	TiO_2	SiO_2	Loss
Actual Percentage Analyses									
*Felspars: Ortho	11.10	2.50	0.20	0.10	0.05	19.40	–	66.00	0.2
* Albite	–	9.1	0.8	–	0.15	20.5	–	67.2	2.1
Anorthite	1.62	0.14	17.01	0.72	1.20	33.75	0.14	45.10	0.31
*Cornish Stone	4.60	1.96	0.94	0.09	0.20	18.64	0.09	70.25	3.01
*Nepheline Syenite	5.20	10.50	0.40	–	0.06	23.30	–	60.10	0.5
†Spodumene (Li_2O = 6.78)	0.69	0.46	0.11	0.13	0.53	28.42	–	62.91	0.28
*China Clay	0.86	0.74	0.78	0.11	0.32	37.74	0.14	46.32	12.52
*Dolomite	0.04	0.11	31.41	20.77	0.04	0.56	–	1.04	42.8
*Whiting	–	–	55.09	0.25	0.10	0.02	–	0.19	44.35
‡Steatite (Talc)	–	–	0.26	31.28	2.91	0.54	0.03	58.10	6.57
*Flint	0.05	0.05	1.01	trace	0.14	0.22	0.02	97.54	1.30
Lead Monosilicate (PbO = 78.7)								21.3	
Bisilicate (PbO = 63.0)	0.3	0.1	0.5	0.1	0.2	0.7	0.8	34.1	0.2
Sesquisilicate (PbO = 68.9)	0.4	0.1	0.3	0.2	0.3	1.3	1.2	26.3	0.3
Theoretical Analyses									
Felspars: Ortho	16					18		65	
Albite		12				19		68	
Anorthite			20			37		43	
Cornish Stone	5		2			18		75	
Nepheline Syenite	5	10.5	0.5			24		60	
Spodumene	8 (Li_2O)					27		65	
China Clay						40		46	14
Dolomite			30	22					48
Whiting			56						44
Steatite (Talc)				32				63	5
Flint								100	
Lead Monosilicate	$\dfrac{PbO}{78}$							22	
Bisilicate	65							35	
Sesquisilicate	69							31	

*Typical analyses provided by W. Podmore and Sons, Ltd., Caledonian Mills, Shelton, Stoke-on-Trent, England. True only for the batch in question.

†From *Journal of the American Ceramic Society*. 21:189 (1938).

‡From *H.M.S.O. (Lond) Chemical Analyses of Igneous Rocks. 1956.*

TABLE I. COMPARISON OF PERCENTAGES OF FLUX, ALUMINA AND SILICA IN TYPICAL GLAZES AND CERAMIC MATERIALS

	Flux approx. %	Alumina approx. %	Silica approx. %	Loss approx. %
Glaze Materials				
China Clay	2.5	38	46.5	13
Cornish Stone	8	19	70	3
Orthoclase Felspar	14	19.5	66	0.5
Soda Felspar	10	21	67	2
Lead Bisilicate	64	1	34.5	0.5
Lead Sesquisilicate	70	2	27.5	0.5
Typical Glazes				
900°C	56	7	37	
1000°C	50	8.5	41.5	
1100°C	47	8	45	
1200°C	41	8	51	
1300°C	15.5	14.5	70	
1400°C	10	14.5	75.5	
Clays and Bodies				
Red Clay	9.5	22	61	7.5
Ball Clay	2.5	39	45	13.5
Stoneware Clay	6	27	59	8
Chinese Porcelain	6	23	71	
Soft Paste Porcelain	29	6	65	
Bone China	29	18	53	
Glasses				
Pyrex Glass	17.5	2	80.5	
Window Glass	27.5	0.5	72	
Glass Cloth Fibre	22	14	64	
Others				
Enamel for Sheet Iron	30	12	58	
Portland Cement	65 (CaO)	7 $+3Fe_2O_3$	23	2(SO_3)

TABLE J. RECIPES BY WEIGHT FROM SEGER'S PAPER ON STANDARD CONES
(Those below 1100°C. and above 1790°C. have been added since.)

Cone No.	Felspar	Marble	Quartz	Iron Oxide	Zettlitz Kaolin
1	83.55	35	66	16.0	–
3	83.55	35	57	4.0	19.43
5	83.55	35	84	–	25.90
7	83.55	35	132	–	51.80
9	83.55	35	180	–	77.70
11	83.55	35	252	–	116.55
13	83.55	35	348	–	168.35
15	83.55	35	468	–	233.10
17	83.55	35	612	–	310.80
19	83.55	35	804	–	414.4
27	83.55	35	4764	–	2551.13
35	Zettlitz Kaolin				
36	Rackonitz Shale Clay				

Note on the Use of Cones: Temperature-recording cones are 2½" high. They are triangular in section, tapering towards the top. They are set in a pad of clay in view of the spyhole of the kiln with the back edge (opposite the number) vertical. When the kiln approaches the temperature specified, the cone begins to bend and the final temperature is reached when the tip has bent over so that it is level with the base. If the heating continues well above the bending point, the cone will melt into a pool of glass.

The bending point is to some extent influenced by the speed of the firing. In this respect cones record the condition of the ware inside the kiln more accurately than a pyrometer which shows only the temperature. Cones containing lead oxide are badly affected by reduction fumes.

Originally all cones were referred to as Seger cones after their inventor (see page 25) but they are now manufactured by several companies and named accordingly.

TABLE K. CORRELATIONS AND TYPICAL COMPOSITIONS OF PYROMETRIC CONES

European Seger Cone Numbers	Bending Point °C.	American Orton Cones* °C.		Typical Molecular Ratios					
				Na_2O	PbO	Al_2O_3	SiO_2	B_2O_3	Fe_2O_3
022	600°	022	(605°)	0.5	0.5	–	2	1	–
021	650°	020	(650°)	0.5	0.5	0.1	2.2	1	–
018	710°	018	(720°)	0.5	0.5	0.4	2.8	1	–
016	750°	017	(770°)	0.5	0.5	0.55	3	1	–
014A	815°	014	(830°)	0.5	0.5	0.65	3.3	1	–
012A	855°	013	(860°)	0.5	0.5	0.75	3.5	1	–
				K_2O	CaO				
010A	900°	010	(895°)	0.3	0.7	0.3	3.5	0.45	0.2
08A	940°	08	(950°)	0.3	0.7	0.3	3.6	0.40	0.2
06A	980°	07	(990°)	0.3	0.7	0.3	3.7	0.3	0.2
04A	1020°	05	(1040°)	0.3	0.7	0.3	3.8	0.2	0.2
02A	1060°	04	(1060°)	0.3	0.7	0.3	3.9	0.1	0.2
1A	1100°	03	(1115°)	0.3	0.7	0.3	4	–	0.2
3A	1140°	01	(1145°)	0.3	0.7	0.45	4	–	0.05
5A	1180°	4	(1190°)	0.3	0.7	0.5	5	–	–
7	1230°	6	(1230°)	0.3	0.7	0.7	7	–	–
9	1280°	9	(1285°)	0.3	0.7	0.9	9	–	–
11	1320°	11	(1325°)	0.3	0.7	1.2	12	–	–
13	1380°	13	(1400°)	0.3	0.7	1.6	16	–	–
15	1435°	15	(1435°)	0.3	0.7	2.1	21	–	–
17	1480°	18	(1490°)	0.3	0.7	2.7	27	–	–
19	1520°	19	(1520°)	0.3	0.7	3.5	35	–	–
27	1610°	27	(1605°)	0.3	0.7	20	20	–	–
32	1710°	32	(1700°)	–	–	1	4	–	–
36	1790°	35	(1785°)	–	–	1	2	–	–
40	1920°	40	(1885°)	–	–	1	0.66	–	–
42	2000°		(2015°)	–	–	1	–	–	–

*Orton cones are quoted for two different rates of firing and the numbers given above represent the nearest points on the 150° of temperature rise per hour scale. The figures in brackets show the actual temperatures quoted for the cones in degrees centigrade.

TABLE L. REFERENCE LIST OF MOLECULAR WEIGHTS

Elements	Oxides Entering Glaze Compositions	Molecular Weight	Compounds Prior to Fusion in Glazes	Molecular Weight
Aluminium	Al_2O_3	102		
Antimony	Sb_2O_3	291.6		
Barium	BaO	153.3	$BaCO_3$	197.3
Boron	B_2O_3	69.6		
Cadmium	CdO	128.4		
Calcium	CaO	56.1	$CaCO_3$	100.1
Carbon			CO_2	44
			CO_3	60
Chlorine			Cl_2	71
Chromium	Cr_2O_3	152		
Cobalt	CoO	74.9	$CoCO_3$	118.9
Copper	CuO	79.5	Cu_2O	143
Hydrogen			H_2O	18
Iron	Fe_2O_3	159.8	FeO	71.9
Lead	PbO	223.2	Pb_3O_4	685.6
Lithium	Li_2O	29.8	Li_2CO_3	73.8
Magnesium	MgO	40.3	$MgCO_3$	84.3
Manganese	MnO	70.9	MnO_2	96.9
Nickel	NiO	74.7	Ni_2O_3	165.4
Nitrogen			NO_3	62
Phosphorus	P_2O_5	142	PO_4	95
Potassium	K_2O	94.2	K_2CO_3	138.2
Silicon	SiO_2	60.1		
Silver	Ag_2O	231.8		
Sodium	Na_2O	62	Na_2CO_3	106
Strontium	SrO	103.6	$SrCO_3$	147.6
Sulphur			SO_2	64.1
			SO_4	96.1
Tin	SnO_2	150.7		
Titanium	TiO_2	79.9		
Uranium	UO_2	270		
Vanadium	V_2O_5	261.8		
Zinc	ZnO	81.4	$ZnCO_3$	125.4
Zirconium	ZrO_2	123.2	$ZrSiO_4$	183.3

Note: Molecular weights are obtained by adding together the atomic weights of the atoms combined in the formula of the substance. The list above will be useful for quickly determining the molecular weights of the minerals listed in Table M.

Notes: Oxides which enter into glaze compositions and to which all other compounds break down on heating are underlined in the formulas column. Common pottery substances appear in capital letters.

*For aluminum, barium, calcium, lithium, potassium, silicon, and sodium see also aluminum silicates at the end of the table, page 136.

†For cobalt, iron, lead, magnesium, silicon, sodium, zinc, and zirconium see also silicates at the end of the table, page 136.

Chemical Names	Formulas	Mineral Names	Other Names: Trade and Trivial
ALUMINIUM* oxide (ALUMINA)	$\underline{Al_2O_3}$	corundum: ruby, sapphire, oriental amethyst, oriental emerald, and oriental topaz	emery (with magnetite and hematite)
hydrated oxides:	$Al_2O_3 \cdot H_2O$	diaspore and boehmite	—
	$Al_2O_3 \cdot 2H_2O$	BAUXITE	—
	$Al_2O_3 \cdot 3H_2O$	gibbsite and hydrargillite	—
sulphates:	$Al_2O_3 \cdot SO_3 \cdot 9H_2O$	websterite and aluminite	—
	$Al_2O_3 \cdot 3SO_3 \cdot 16H_2O$	alunogene	—
with ammonium	$Al_2(SO_4)_3 (NH_4)_2 SO_4 \cdot 24H_2O$	—	alum (ammonium)
with potassium	$Al_2(SO_4)_3 K_2SO_4 \cdot 24H_2O$	—	alum (potassium)
fluoride	$AlF_3 \cdot 3NaF$	CRYOLITE	—
ANTIMONY oxides: (trioxide)	$\underline{Sb_2O_3}$	senarmontite and valentinite	—
(tetroxide)	$\underline{Sb_2O_4}$	—	antimony ochre
	$Sb_2O_3 \cdot Sb_2O_5$	cervantite and kermesite	red antimony
chloride (trichloride)	$SbCl_3$	—	butter of antimony
sulphide (trisulphide)	Sb_2S_3	antimonite and STIBNITE	antimony glance and gray antimony
BARIUM* oxides: (BARIA)	$\underline{BaO}$	—	—
(peroxide)	BaO_2	—	—
(hydroxide)	$Ba(OH)_2$	—	—
carbonates	$BaCO_3$	WITHERITE	—
double carbonates	$(Ba, Ca)CO_3$	bromlite and alstonite	—
	$BaCo_3 \cdot CaCO_3$	barytocalcite	—
chloride	$BaCl_2 \cdot 2H_2O$	—	—
sulphate	$BaSO_4$	barytes, heavy spar, and barite	Bologna stone, caulk, cawk stone, calk stone, and fixed white
chromate	$BaCrO_4$	—	—
selenite	$BaO \cdot SeO_2$	—	—

Chemical Names	Formulas	Mineral Names	Other Names: Trade and Trivial
BISMUTH			
oxide (trioxide)	Bi_2O_3	bismite	bismuth ochre
carbonate (basic)	$Bi_2CO_3 \cdot H_2O$	bismutite	—
BORON			
oxides:	B_2O_3	—	—
(hydrous)	$B(OH)_3$	sassolite	—
borates: hydrated sodium	$Na_2O \cdot 2B_2O_3 \cdot 10H_2O$	borax	BORAX and tincal
(tetraborate or diborate)	$Na_2O \cdot 2B_2O_3 \cdot 4H_2O$	kernite	—
hydrated calcium	$2CaO \cdot 3B_2O_3 \cdot 5H_2O$	COLEMANITE	—
hydrated sodium and calcium	$Na_2O \cdot 2CaO \cdot 5B_2O_3 \cdot 16H_2O$	ulexite	—
acid (boric acid or orthoboric acid)	H_3BO_3	—	BORACIC ACID and sedative salts
CADMIUM			
oxide	CdO	—	—
carbonate	$CdCO_3$	—	—
sulphate	$CdSO_4$	—	—
sulphide	CdS	greenockite	—
CALCIUM*			
oxides: (CALCIA)	CaO	LIME	quicklime (when fresh)
hydroxide	$Ca(OH)_2$	—	hydrated lime and slaked lime
carbonates:	$CaCO_3$	calcite, calc spar, chalk, Iceland spar, limestone, marble, aragonite, and bath stone	Paris white and WHITING
double carbonates	$CaCO_3 \cdot MgCO_3$	DOLOMITE	—
	$Na_2CO_3 \cdot CaCO_3 \cdot 5H_2O$	gaylussite	—
	$BaCO_3 \cdot CaCO_3$	barytocalcite	—
chlorides: (anhydrous)	$CaCl_2$	—	—
(hydrous)	$CaCl_2 \cdot 6H_2O$	—	
	$CaO \cdot Cl_2$	—	chloride of lime and bleaching powder
nitrate	$Ca(NO_3)_2$	—	wall saltpeter
sulphates:	$CaSO_4$	anhydrite	—
	$CaSO_4 \cdot 2H_2O$	gypsum, alabaster, and selenite	—
	$(CaSO_4)_2 \cdot H_2O$	—	PLASTER OF PARIS

Chemical Names	Formulas	Mineral Names	Other Names: Trade and Trivial
with sodium	$Na_2SO_4 \cdot CaSO_4$	glauberite	–
with potassium and magnesium	$K_2SO_4 \cdot MgSO_4 \cdot 2CaSO_4$	polyhalite	–
borate	$2CaO \cdot 3B_2O_3 \cdot 5H_2O$	COLEMANITE	–
fluoride	CaF_2	fluorspar, Derbyshire spar, and fluorite	"Blue John"
phosphates (ortho)	$Ca_3(PO_4)_2$	–	BONE ASH or calcined bone
superphosphate	$Ca_3(PO_4)_2 \cdot CaSO_4$	–	–
chlorophosphate	$3Ca_3(PO_4)_2 \cdot Ca(Cl, F)_2$	apatite	–
CARBON			
native element	C	diamond and graphite	–
with hydrogen	C_XH_X	coal, petroleum, bitumen, asphalt, pitch, and amber	–
oxides: monoxide	CO	–	–
dioxide	CO_2	–	–
acid (carbonic)	H_2CO_3	–	–
CHROMIUM			
oxide: sesqui	Cr_2O_3	–	–
oxide of chrome and iron	$FeO \cdot Cr_2O_3$	CHROMITE	chrome iron ore
sulphate	$Cr_2(SO_4)_3 \cdot 18H_2O$	–	–
chrome alum	$Cr_2(SO_4)_2K_2SO_4 \cdot 24H_2O$	–	–
phosphate: ortho	$Cr(PO_4) \cdot 2H_2O$	–	–
lead chromate	$Pb \cdot Cr \cdot O_4$	crocoite	CHROME YELLOW
COBALT†			
oxides: cobaltous (gray)	CoO	–	–
cobaltic (gray-black)	Co_2O_3	–	–
cobalto-cobaltic (black)	Co_3O_4 or $Co_3O_3 \cdot CoO$	–	–
with manganese mixture	cobalt up to 50%	asbolite and asbolan	earthy cobalt and black oxide of cobalt
carbonate: cobaltous	$CoCO_3$	–	–
chlorides: cobaltic	Co_2Cl_6	–	–
cobaltous hydrated	$CoCl_2 \cdot 6H_2O$	–	–
nitrate: cobaltous	$Co(NO_3)_2 \cdot 6H_2O$	–	–

Chemical Names	Formulas	Mineral Names	Other Names: Trade and Trivial
sulphates: cobaltous	$CoSO_4 \cdot 7H_2O$	—	—
anhydrous	$CoSO_4$	—	—
sulphide	Co_3S_4	linnaeite	cobalt glance
arsenide	$CoAs_2$	SMALTITE and smaltine	tin white cobalt
sulpharsenide	$CoAsS$	COBALTITE	—
arsenate: hydrated	$Co_3As_2O_8 \cdot 8H_2O$	erythrite	cobalt bloom
phosphate	$Co_3(PO_4)_2 \cdot 8H_2O$	—	—
glasses	—	—	smalt and zaffre
COPPER			
oxides: cuprous	Cu_2O	CUPRITE and chalcotrichite	red oxide of copper
cupric	CuO	tenorite and melaconite	black oxide of copper
hydroxides: cuprous	$4Cu_2O \cdot H_2O$	—	—
cupric	$Cu(OH)_2$	—	—
carbonates: basic hydrated	$CuCO_3 \cdot Cu(OH)_2$	MALACHITE	—
	$2CuCO_3 \cdot Cu(OH)_2$	AZURITE	blue carbonate of copper
chloride: cuprous	Cu_2Cl_2	—	—
cupric	$CuCl_2 \cdot 2H_2O$	—	—
oxychloride, hydrated	$CuCl_2 \cdot 3Cu(OH)_2$	atacamite and remolinite	—
nitrate	$Cu(NO_3)_2 \cdot 6H_2O$	—	—
sulphates: cuprous	Cu_2SO_4	—	—
cupric (hydrated)	$CuSO_4 \cdot 5H_2O$	chalcanthite and cyanosite	blue vitriol and copper vitriol
(anhydrous)	$CuSO_4$	—	—
basic	$Cu_3(SO_4)(OH)_4$	antlerite	—
with lead	$PbCu(SO_4)(OH)_2$	linarite	—
sulphides: cuprous	Cu_2S	chalcocite and redruthite	copper glance and vitreous copper ore
cupric	CuS	covelline and covellite	—
with iron	$Cu_2S \cdot Fe_2S_3$	chalcopyrite	copper pyrites
	Cu_3FeS_3	bornite and erubescite	variegated copper ore
GOLD			
chloride	$AuCl_3$	—	auric chloride
HYDROGEN			
oxide	H_2O	WATER	—

Chemical Names	Formulas	Mineral Names	Other Names: Trade and Trivial
chloride	HCl	—	hydrochloric acid, spirits of salts, and muriatic acid
nitrate	HNO_3	—	nitric acid and aqua fortis
sulphates	H_2SO_4	—	sulphuric acid, oil of vitriol, and vitriol
	H_2SO_3	—	sulphurous acid
fluoride	HF	—	hydrofluoric acid
phosphates	H_3PO_3	—	phosphorous acid
	H_3PO_4	—	phosphoric acid
IRON†			
oxides: ferrous	FeO	—	—
ferric	$\underline{Fe_2O_3}$	HAEMATITE (HEMATITE), martite, colcothar, and kidney ore	crocus martis, rouge, Indian red, and specular iron
ferroso-ferric (triferric tetroxide)	Fe_3O_4	MAGNETITE, loadstone or lodestone	magnetic oxide of iron and iron scale
hydrated oxides:			
ferric	$Fe_2O_3 \cdot H_2O$	goethite	—
	$2Fe_2O_3 \cdot H_2O$	turgite	—
	$2Fe_2O_3 \cdot 3H_2O$	limonite	brown hematite
ferrous	$FeO(OH)$	lepidocrocite	—
with chrome	$FeCr_2O_4$ (ferrous chromate)	chromite	chrome ironstone
	$Fe_2(Cr_2O_7)_3$ (ferric dichromate)	—	—
carbonate: ferrous	$FeCO_3$	SIDERITE, chalybite	spathic iron ore and sapphire quartz
chloride: ferric	Fe_2Cl_6	—	—
sulphates: ferrous	$FeSO_4 \cdot 7H_2O$	copperas and melanterite	green vitriol
ferric	$Fe_2(SO_4)_3 \cdot 9H_2O$	—	—
sulphides: ferrous	FeS	—	—
ferric	FeS_2 (iron disulphide)	IRON PYRITES, mundic, and marcasite	fools gold and white iron pyrites
	Fe_xS_{x+1}	pyrrhotite and pyrrhotine	magnetic pyrites
phosphates: ferric	$FePO_4 \cdot 2H_2O$	—	—
(hydrated)	$Fe_3P_2O_8 \cdot 8H_2O$	vivianite	blue iron earth
iron alum	$Fe_2(SO_4)_3(NH_4)_2SO_4 \cdot 24H_2O$	—	—
LEAD†			
oxides: monoxide	$\underline{PbO}$	—	LITHARGE
dioxide	PbO_2	—	brown oxide of lead
tetroxide (triplumbic)	Pb_3O_4 or $2PbO \cdot PbO_2$	minium and mennige	RED LEAD

Chemical Names	Formulas	Mineral Names	Other Names: Trade and Trivial
carbonates:	$PbCO_3$	CERRUSITE	ceruse and white lead ore
basic	$2PbCO_3 \cdot Pb(OH)_2$	hydrocerrusite	white lead, basic
chloride	$PbCl_2$	—	—
chlorocarbonate	$PbCO_3 \cdot PbCl_2$	phosgenite and cromfordite	horn lead
sulphate	$PbSO_4$	anglesite	lead vitriol
suphide	PbS	GALENA	Lead glance and blue lead
borate: metaborate	$PbO \cdot B_2O_3 \cdot H_2O$	—	—
chromate	$PbCrO_4$	crocoite	chrome yellow
Antimoniates: ortho	$Pb_3(SbO_4)_2$	—	Naples yellow
pyro	Pb_2SbO_7	—	—
Sulphatocarbonate:	$PbSO_4 \cdot 2PbCO_3 \cdot Pb(OH)_2$	leadhillite	
LITHIUM*			
oxide (LITHIA)	$\underline{Li_2O}$	—	—
carbonate	Li_2CO_3	—	—
aluminium phosphate	$LiAlPO_4OH$	montebrasite	—
fluophosphate of Li and Al	$LiAlPO_4(FOH)$	amblygonite	
lithium cobaltite	$LiCoO_2$	—	—
MAGNESIUM†			
oxide: (MAGNESIA)	$\underline{MgO}$	periclase and native magnesia	—
hydroxide	$\underline{Mg(OH)_2}$	brucite	—
carbonates:	$MgCO_3$	MAGNESITE	—
double	$MgCO_3 \cdot CaCO_3$	DOLOMITE	—
chlorides	$MgCl_2 \cdot 6H_2O$	—	—
	$MgCl_2 \cdot KCl \cdot 6H_2O$	carnallite	—
sulphates: hydrated	$MgSO_4 \cdot 2H_2O$	kieserite	—
	$MgSO_4 \cdot 7H_2O$	epsomite	epsom salts
	$MgSO_4 \cdot K_2SO_4 \cdot 2CaSO_4 \cdot 2H_2O$	polyhalite	—
	$MgSO_4 \cdot KCl \cdot 3H_2O$	kainite	—
aluminate	$MgAl_2O_4$	spinel	—
phosphate	$Mg_3(PO_4)_2$	—	—

Chemical Names	Formulas	Mineral Names	Other Names: Trade and Trivial
MANGANESE			
oxides: manganous	$\underline{MnO}$	manganosite	—
dioxide	MnO_2	PYROLUSITE and polianite	black oxide of manganese
trioxide	Mn_2O_3	BRAUNITE	—
tetroxide	Mn_3O_4	hausmannite	—
(trimanganic)			
Hydrated oxides (with K + Na + Ba)	mixture	psilomelane	wad (various naturally occurring mixtures of oxides)
	$MnO(OH)$	manganite	—
carbonate: manganous	$MnCO_3$	rhodocrosite and diallogite	—
chloride: manganous	$MnCl_2 \cdot 4H_2O$	—	—
sulphates: manganous	$MnSO_4 \cdot 4H_2O$	—	—
manganic	$Mn_2(SO_4)_3$	—	—
sulphide: manganous	MnS	alabandite	—
phosphates: ortho	$MnPO_4 \cdot H_2O$	—	—
monohydrogen	$MnHPO_4 \cdot 3H_2O$	—	—
NICKEL			
oxides: nickelous	$\underline{NiO}$	—	gray oxide
nickelic	Ni_2O_3	—	black oxide
carbonate	$NiCO_3 \cdot 2Ni(OH)_2 \cdot 4H_2O$	zaratite	emerald nickel
chlorides:	$NiCl_2$	—	—
hydrated:	$NiCl_2 \cdot 6H_2O$	—	—
sulphates:	$NiSO_4$	—	
	$NiSO_4 \cdot 7H_2O$	morenosite	nickel vitriol
sulphides	NiS	millerite	nickel pyrites, capillary pyrites, and hair pyrites
with iron	$(FeNi)S$	pentlandite	—
POTASSIUM*			
oxide: (POTASH or POTASSA)	$\underline{K_2O}$	—	potash (incorrectly) potassa
hydroxide	KOH	—	potash, caustic potash, and caustic alkali
carbonates:	K_2CO_3	—	potashes
bicarbonate	$KHCO_3$	—	PEARL ASH, salt of tartar, and bicarbonate of potash
chlorides:	KCl	sylvine and sylvite	Stassfurt salts
hydrated with Mg	$KCl \cdot MgCl_2 \cdot 6H_2O$	carnallite	—
hydrated with Mg	$KCl \cdot MgSO_4 \cdot 3H_2O$	kainite	—

Chemical Names	Formulas	Mineral Names	Other Names: Trade and Trivial
nitrate	KNO_3	nitre	saltpetre and nitrate of potash
sulphates: with Al	$K_2O \cdot 3Al_2O_3 \cdot 4SO_3 \cdot 6H_2O$	alunite	alumstone
with Mg & Ca	$K_2SO_4 \cdot MgSO_4 \cdot 2CaSO_4 \cdot 2H_2O$	polyhalite	–
with H bisulphate	$KHSO_4$	–	bisulphate of potash
with Al	$Al_2(SO_4)_3 \cdot K^2SO_4 \cdot 24H_2O$	alum	potash alum
sulphide	K_2S	–	liver of sulphur
chromates:	K_2CrO_4	–	–
dichromate	K_2CrO_7	–	potassium bichromate
antimoniates: meta	$KSbO_3 \cdot xH_2O$	–	–
pyro	$K_2H_2Sb_2O_7 \cdot 4H_2O$	–	–
permanganate	$KMnO_4$	–	–
SILICON*†			
oxide: dioxide (SILICA)	$\underline{SiO_2}$	SILICA, rock crystal, QUARTZ, FLINT, chert, cristobalite, tridymite, SAND, lynn sand, silver sand, QUARTZITE, agate, aventurine, jasper, amethyst, chalcedony, and ganister	silex (ancient name)
carbide	SiC	corundum	–
fluoride	SiF_4	–	–
acid	K_2SiO_3	–	silicilic acid
SILVER			
oxide	$\underline{Ag_2O}$	–	–
carbonate	Ag_2CO_3	–	–
nitrate	$AgNO_3$	–	lunar caustic
chloride	$AgCl$	cerargyrite and kerargyrite	horn silver
sulphide	Ag_2S	argentite	silver glance
SODIUM*†			
oxide: (SODA)	$\underline{Na_2O}$	–	–
hydroxide	$NaOH$	–	caustic soda

Chemical Names	Formulas	Mineral Names	Other Names: Trade and Trivial
carbonates:			
anhydrous	Na_2CO_3	–	SODA ASH and black ash
hydrated	$Na_2CO_3 \cdot 10H_2O$	natron	soda crystals and washing soda
hydrated	$Na_2CO_3 \cdot H_2O$	thermonatrite	–
bicarbonate	$NaHCO_3$	–	–
hydrated basic	$Na_2CO_3 \cdot NaHCO_3 \cdot 2H_2O$	trona and urao	.–
with calcium	$Na_2CO_3 \cdot CaCO_3 \cdot 5H_2O$	gaylussite	–
chlorides:	$NaCl$	HALITE and rock salt	salt and COMMON SALT
hypochloride	$NaClO$	–	–
nitrate	$NaNO_3$	Soda-nitre and nitratine	nitrate of soda and Chile saltpetre
Sulphates:	Na_2SO_4	thenardite	saltcake
hyposulphite	$Na_2S_2O_3 \cdot 5H_2O$	–	antichlor
hydrated	$Na_2SO_4 \cdot 10H_2O$	mirabilite	Glauber salt
with calcium	$Na_2SO_4 \cdot CaSO_4$	glauberite	–
sulphide	Na_2S	–	–
chromates:	$Na_2CrO_4 \cdot 10H_2O$	–	–
dichromate	$Na_2Cr_2O_7 \cdot 2H_2O$	–	–
aluminium fluoride:	Na_3AlF_6	cryolite and Greenland spar	–
selenate	$Na_2O \cdot SeO_3$	–	–
selenite	$Na_2O \cdot SeO_2 \cdot 5H_2O$	–	–
stannate	$Na_2SnO_3 \cdot 3H_2O$	–	–
uranate:	$Na_2U_2O_7$	–	yellow uranium oxide
TIN			
oxides: stannous	SnO	–	–
stannic	$\underline{SnO_2}$	CASSITERITE and tinstone	terrar, stannolite (both substitutes), and putty powder
chlorides: stannous	$SnCl_2 \cdot 2H_2O$	–	butter of tin
stannic	$SnCl_4$	–	–
sulphides:	SnS_2	–	mosaic gold
with copper and iron	$SnS_2 \cdot Cu_2S \cdot FeS$	stannine and tin pyrites	bell metal ore
STRONTIUM			
oxide (STRONTIA)	$\underline{SrO}$	–	–
carbonate	$SrCO_3$	strontianite	–

Chemical Names	Formulas	Mineral Names	Other Names: Trade and Trivial
sulphate	$SrSO_4$	celestine and celestite	—
chromate	$SrCrO_4$	—	—
SULPHUR			
oxides: dioxide	SO_2	—	—
trioxide	SO_3	—	—
TITANIUM			
oxides: dioxide (TITANIA)	TiO_2	anatase, brookite, octo-hedrite, and RUTILE (impure—with iron)	—
with iron	$FeO \cdot TiO_2$	ILMENITE and menaccanite	—
TUNGSTEN			
oxide	WO_3	tungstite and tungstic ochre	—
tungstates	$(Fe, Mn)WO_4$	wolfram and WOLFRAMITE	—
URANIUM			
oxides: uranous	$\underline{UO_2}$	—	—
uranyl	$\overline{UO_3}$	—	—
uranyl uranate	$UO_2 \cdot 2UO_3$ or U_3O_8	pitchblende and uraninite	—
VANADIAM			
oxide: pentoxide	$\underline{V_2O_5}$	patronite	—
sulphide	VS_4	—	—
chlorovanadate of lead	$3Pb_3V_2O_8 \cdot PbCl_2$	—	—
ZINC†			
oxides:	ZnO	zincite, spartalite, and sterlingite	red oxide of zinc and philosophers wool
with variable iron and manganese	$(Fe, Zn, Mn)O \cdot (Fe, Mn)_2O_3$	franklinite	—
carbonates:	$ZnCO_3$	smithsonite and calamine	—
basic	$2ZnCO_3 \cdot 3Zn(OH)_2$	hydrozincite	—
sulphate	$ZnSO_4 \cdot 7H_2O$	goslarite	white vitriol
sulphide	ZnS	blende, SPHALERITE, and wurtzite	"blackjack"
aluminate	$ZnO \cdot Al_2O_3$	gahnite	zinc spinel
chromate	$ZnCrO_4$	—	—
ZIRCONIUM			
oxide	$\underline{ZrO_2}$	baddeleyite	zirconite (general term for various zircon minerals)

Chemical Names	Formulas	Mineral Names	Other Names: Trade and Trivial
SILICATES			
calcium	$CaO \cdot SiO_2$	WOLLASTONITE	tabular spar
calcium and magnesium	$CaO \cdot MgO \cdot SiO_2$	diopside	–
cobalt(ous)	Co_2SiO_4	–	–
iron	Fe_2SiO_4	fayalite	iron olivine
lead: MONO	$PbO \cdot SiO_2$	–	–
BISILICATE	$PbO \cdot 2SiO_2$	(manufactured)	–
SESQUISILICATE	$2PbO \cdot 3SiO_2$	–	–
magnesium	$MgO \cdot SiO_2$	enstatite	–
	$2MgO \cdot SiO_2$	forsterite	magnesian olivine
magnesian (hydrous)	$3MgO \cdot 2SiO_2 \cdot 2H_2O$	serpentine	–
magnesium and iron	$(Fe, Mg)O \cdot SiO_2$	hypersthene	–
magnesium and iron (orthosilicate)	$2(Mg, Fe)O \cdot SiO_2$	peridot, olivine, and chrysolite	–
magnesian: (hydrous meta silicate)	$3MgO \cdot 4SiO_2 \cdot 2H_2O$	TALC and STEATITE	–
(hydrous)	$3MgO \cdot 4SiO_2 \cdot xH_2O$	vermiculite	–
manganese	$MnO \cdot SiO_2$	rhodonite	manganese spar
sodium	$2Na_2O \cdot SiO_2$	–	waterglass
sodium and iron meta silicate	$2Na \cdot Fe(SiO_3) \cdot FeSiO_3$	riebeckite	–
zinc (ortho)	$2ZnO \cdot SiO_2$	willemite (wilhelmite)	–
zircon	$ZrSiO_4$	ZIRCON	–
ALUMINIUM SILICATES			
	$Al_2O_3 \cdot SiO_2$	andalusite	–
	$Al_2O_3 \cdot SiO_2$	SILLIMANITE and fibrolite	–
	$Al_2O_3 \cdot SiO_2$	kyanite, cyanite, and disthene	–
	$3Al_2O_3 \cdot 2SiO_2$	mullite	–
aluminium fluosilicate	$Al_2F_2 \cdot SiO_4$	topaz	–
hydrated aluminum silicates	$Al_2O_3 \cdot 2SiO_2 \cdot 2H_2O$	kaolinite, nacrite, dickite, KAOLIN, and halloysite	CHINA CLAY
	$Al_2O_3 \cdot 3SiO_2 \cdot 4H_2O$	beidellite	–
	$Al_2O_3 \cdot 4SiO_2 \cdot H_2O$	pyrophillite	–

Chemical Names	Formulas	Mineral Names	Other Names: Trade and Trivial

ALUMINIUM SILICATES WITH OTHER METALS

FELSPARS:

Chemical Names	Formulas	Mineral Names	Other Names: Trade and Trivial
barium	$BaO \cdot Al_2O_3 \cdot 2SiO_2$	celsian	–
potassium	$K_2O \cdot Al_2O_3 \cdot 6SiO_2$	ORTHOCLASE and microline	–
sodium	$Na_2O \cdot Al_2O_3 \cdot 6SiO_2$	ALBITE and barbierite	–
calcium	$CaO \cdot Al_2O_3 \cdot 2SiO_2$	anorthite and indianite	–

MIXED FELSPARS:

Chemical Names	Formulas	Mineral Names	Other Names: Trade and Trivial
barium and potassium	celsian and orthoclase in varying proportions	hyalophane	–
potassium and sodium	orthoclase and albite in varying proportions	soda-orthoclase, anorthoclase, and soda microline	moonstone (very little albite)
sodium and calcium (the plagioclase felspars)	albite with up to 30% anorthite	oligoclase	–
	albite with up to 50% anorthite	andesine	–
	albite with up to 70% anorthite	labradorite	–
	albite with up to 90% anorthite	bytownite	–

FELSPATHOIDS:

(felspars deficient in silica)

Chemical Names	Formulas	Mineral Names	Other Names: Trade and Trivial
sodium	$Na_2O \cdot Al_2O_3 \cdot 2SiO_2$	nepheline and nephelite	(NEPHELINE SYENITE is a mixture of nepheline and alkali felspars)
potassium	$K_2O \cdot Al_2O_3 \cdot 4SiO_2$	leucite	–
sodium, with sodium chloride	$3(Na_2O \cdot Al_2O_3 \cdot 2SiO_2) \cdot 2NaCl$	sodalite	–

MICAS:

Chemical Names	Formulas	Mineral Names	Other Names: Trade and Trivial
potassium	$K_2O \cdot 3Al_2O_3 \cdot 6SiO_2 \cdot 2H_2O$	muscovite	common mica and Muscovy glass
potassium and lithium	$K(Li \cdot Al)_3 \cdot (Si, Al)_4O_{10}$ $(F \cdot OH)_2$ (variable)	LEPIDOLITE	lithia mica
potassium, magnesium and iron	$K(Mg, Fe)_3(Al, Si)_3O_{10}$ $(OH)_2$ (variable)	biotite	–
sodium	$Na_2O \cdot 3Al_2O_3 \cdot 6SiO_2 \cdot 2H_2O$	paragonite	sodium mica

OTHERS:

Chemical Names	Formulas	Mineral Names	Other Names: Trade and Trivial
hydrated, with iron and magnesium	$5(Mg, Fe)O \cdot Al_2O_3 \cdot 3SiO_2 \cdot 4H_2O$	chlorite	–
hydrated, with magnesium	$Al_2O_3 \cdot 5SiO_2 \cdot xH_2O$ $(Mg,Ca)O$	montmorillonite	–
lithium	$Li_2O \cdot Al_2O_3 \cdot 8SiO_2$	PETALITE	Not strictly felspars, but sometimes included with them in ceramic lists
lithium	$Li_2O \cdot Al_2O_3 \cdot 4SiO_2$	SPODUMENE and triphane	

Suggested Reading

Background Studies

Amaldi, Ginestra. *The Nature of Matter*. Chicago: University of Chicago Press, 1965; London: Allen & Unwin, 1966. A clear account illustrated with some plates and diagrams.

Chedd, G. *Half-Way Elements*. New York: Doubleday & Co., Inc.; London: Aldus Books, 1969. Fascinating account of the nature and use of elements; well illustrated.

Feinberg, J.G., and Soddy, F. *The Story of Atomic Theory and Atomic Energy*. New York: Dover Publications, 1960. Soddy discovered isotopes in 1910.

Frisch, O. *The Nature of Matter*. London: Thames & Hudson, 1972. Otto Frisch was the first man to comprehend the processes involved in splitting atoms, and in 1939 he coined the phrase "nuclear fission." A profusely illustrated book.

Hoyle, F. *The Nature of the Universe*. New York: Signet (science paperback), 1955. First published in England in 1950, republished as a Penguin Book in 1960 and frequently reprinted. Brief and very readable.

Isaacs, A. *Introducing Science*. Baltimore: Pelican Books, 1963. Clear and brief description of the attributes of matter and energy.

Jeans, J. *The Universe Around Us*. New York: Cambridge Publications (paperback), 1960. One of the best books on the subject; continually revised and reprinted since 1929.

Jungk, R. *Brighter Than 1000 Suns*. New York: Harcourt Brace Jovanovich (paperback), 1971; London: Gollancz & Hart-Davis, 1958 (original German edition, 1956). A vivid biographical account of the work of scientists involved in the discovery of atomic energy between 1920 and the early 1950's. Science, history, politics, and human relations. An important document.

Kilmister, C. *The Nature of the Universe*. New York: E.P. Dutton Co., 1971; London: Thames & Hudson, 1971. Well illustrated and complete.

Marrison, L.W. *Crystals, Diamond and Transistors*. Baltimore: Penguin Books, Inc., 1966. Readable, "non-textbook" account.

Stewart, A.T. *Perpetual Motion: Electrons in Atoms and Crystals*. New York: Doubleday & Co., Inc. (paperback), 1970. Brief and light-hearted account.

Young, J.A. *Elements of General Chemistry*. New Jersey: Prentice Hall, Inc., 1960. Useful general textbook.

General Studies of the Earth

Dury, G. *The Face of the Earth*. Baltimore: Pelican Books, 1959. Frequent reprints with a revision in 1966. Study of the causes of the character of landscapes. Examples mostly chosen from Britain.

Fraser, R. *Understanding the Earth*. Baltimore: Penguin Books, Inc., 1967. Originally published in 1964 as *The Habitable Earth* by Hodder and Stoughton. A study of the nature of the earth as a whole. Many clear diagrams.

Gaskell, T.F. *Physics of the Earth*. New York: Funk and Wagnalls Co., 1971; London: Thames & Hudson, 1970. A theoretical study; clear and well illustrated.

Holmes, A. *The Principles of Physical Geology*. London: Nelson, 1944. One of the standard works on the subject. Substantial, clear and recommended for almost any age group.

Rapport, S. and Wright, Helen (eds.) *The Crust of the Earth*. New York: Signet Science Library, 1955. Several reprints; collection of relevant articles.

Smart, W.M. *The Origin of the Earth*. Baltimore: Pelican Books, 1955. Several reprints and revisions. A record of scientific investigations grouped under the headings "Whence?", "When?" and "How?".

Swinnerton, H.H. *The Earth Beneath Us*. Baltimore: Penguin Books, 1958; London: Muller, 1955. Brief account including the formation of rocks, past climates, and the development of life forms.

Glazes

Griffiths, R., and Radford, C. *Calculations in Ceramics*. Levittown, New York: Transatlantic Arts, Inc., 1967; London: Maclaren, 1965. Textbook with worked examples, etc.

Hetherington, A.L. *Chinese Ceramic Glazes*. London: Cambridge, 1937; London: Commonwealth Press, 1948. A detailed study of iron and copper glazes. Unique and often referred to.

Parmelee, C.W. *Ceramic Glazes*. Boston: Colners Publishing Co., 1968; London: Industrial Publication, Inc., 1948; the most comprehensive study of the subject available.

Rhodes, D. *Clays and Glazes for the Potter*. Philadelphia: Chilton Book Co., 1957; London: Pitman Publishing, 1957. Readable and fairly detailed study; most useful.

Rhodes, D. *Stoneware and Porcelain: The Art of High Fired Ceramics*. Philadelphia: Chilton Book Co., 1959.

Shaw, K. *Ceramic Colours and Pottery Decoration*. New York: American Elsevier Publishing Co., 1972; London: Maclaren, 1962, revised 1968. History, methods, and theory. At the moment, the only book on the subject available.

_____. *Ceramic Glazes*. New York: American Elsevier Publishing Co., 1971. A brief text mostly concerned with industrial glazes with a short section on studio pottery.

Singer, F., and German, W.L. *Ceramic Glazes*. Issued by Borax Consolidated Ltd., 1960. Frequently reprinted. Excellent general account of industrial glazes. Includes many formulas for all temperatures.

Viehweger, F. *Recipe Book 1: For Glazes and Colors*. Coburg: Sprechsaal-Verlag, 1959, 1965. 1000 recipes for colors, glazes, stains, etc. all given in percentages. Parallel English/German text.

Industrial Handbooks with Sections on Glazes

Jackson, G. *Introduction to Whitewares*. New York: American Elsevier Publishing Co., 1970; London: Maclaren, 1969. Brief and genuinely an "introduction."

Newcomb, R. *Ceramic Whitewares*. London: Pitman Publishing, 1947.

Norton, F.H. *Elements of Ceramics*. Reading, Massachusetts: Addison-Wesley Publishing Co., 1952.

Singer, F. and S. *Industrial Ceramics*. New York: Chemical Publishing Co., 1965; London: Chapman Hall, 1963. Dozens of formulas of all kinds.

Koenig and Earhart. *Literature Abstracts of Ceramic Glazes*. Philadelphia: College Offset Press, 1951. From technical journals, etc.

Minerals: Sources and Uses

Bateman, A.M. *Economic Mineral Deposits*. New York: John Wiley & Sons, 1942. Revised and reprinted frequently. A standard work covering the formation, location, and uses of minerals in industry. Particular reference to the U.S.A.

Ernst, W.G. *Earth Materials*. New Jersey: Prentice Hall, Inc., 1969. One volume in a new series of clearly produced textbooks.

Hurlburt, C., Jr. *Minerals and Man*. New York: Random House, Inc., 1970; London: Thames & Hudson, 1969. Contains illustrations of exceptional quality, along with a fascinating text.

Jones, W.R. *Minerals in Industry*. Baltimore: Pelican Books, 1943. Frequent revision and reprints. Most useful; brief study described element by element.

Jones, W.R., and Williams, W.D. *Minerals and Mineral Deposits*. New York: Oxford University Press, 1948 and reprints. Brief overall text.

Pough, F.H. *A Field Guide to Rocks and Minerals*. Boston: Houghton Mifflin Co., 1953; London: Constable, 1970. Classified list with details of behavior, identification, uses, etc. Diagrams of typical crystals and many color illustrations.

Read, H.W. *Rutley's Elements of Mineralogy*, 26th ed., New York: Hafner Publishing Co., 1970; London: Murby & Co., 1970. Standard reference list.

Minerals: Reference

American Geological Institute. *Dictionary of Geological Terms*. New York: Dolphin Reference Books, 1960.

Mason, B. *The Literature of Geology*. American Museum of Natural History, 1953. For details of geological societies, official publications, and books all over the world, entered country by country. America is especially well covered.

Mineral Resources of the U.S.A. Public Affairs Press, Washington, 1948.

Lead Poisoning from Glazes

International Lead Zinc Research Organization (ILZRO). *Lead Glazes for Dinnerware* (Ceramics Manual No. 1.) 1970. Address. ILZRO, 292 Madison Avenue, New York, N.Y. 10017.

Pottery Handbooks with Chapters on Glazes

Billington, Dora. *The Technique of Pottery*. Great Neck, New York: Hearthside Press, Inc., 1964; London: Batsford, 1962, with reprints.

Binns, C.F. *The Potter's Craft*. New York: Van Nostrand-Rheinhold, 1910. Several reprints up to 1967.

Cardew, M. *Pioneer Pottery*. New York: St. Martins Press, Inc., 1967; London: Longmans Green, 1969.

Leach, B. *A Potter's Book*. Levittown, New York: Transatlantic Arts, Inc., 1956; London: Faber & Faber, 1940.

Nelson, G. *Ceramics*. New York: Holt, Rinehart & Winston, 1960, revised and enlarged 1966 and 1972.

Ruscoe, W. *A Manual for the Potter*. London: Tiranti, 1948, paperback reprints.

Sanders, M. *The World of Japanese Ceramics*. Tokyo: Kodanska International, 1966.

Suppliers List

Clays

American Art Clay Company (AMACO)
4717 W. 16th Street, Indianapolis, Indiana 46222

George Fetzer Company
1205 17th Avenue, Columbus, Ohio 43211

Stewart Clay Company, Inc.
133 Mulberry Street, New York, New York 10013

Trinity Ceramic Supply Company
9016 Diplomacy Row, Dallas, Texas 75247

Western Ceramic Supply Company
1601 Howard Street, San Francisco,
California 94103

Jack D. Wolfe Company, Inc.
724 Meeker Avenue, Brooklyn, New York 11222

Kilns

J.T. Abernathy
212 S. State Street, Ann Arbor, Michigan 48108

A.D. Alpine Company, Inc.
1837 Teale Street, Culver City, California 90230

Denver Fire Clay Company
3033 Blake Street, Denver, Colorado 80205

Pereny Equipment Company, Inc.
Dept. CD, 893 Chambers Road,
Columbus, Ohio 43211

Unique Kilns
530 Spruce Street, Trenton, New Jersey 08368

Kiln Furniture and Cones

George Fetzer Company
1205 17th Avenue, Columbus, Ohio, 43211

Edward Orton Jr. Ceramic Foundation
1445 Summit Street, Columbus, Ohio 43211

Glaze Materials and Equipment

American Art Clay Company (AMACO)
4717 W. 16th Street, Indianapolis, Indiana 46222

Brodhead-Garrett Company
4560 E. 17th Street, Cleveland, Ohio 44105

Gare Ceramic Supply
165 Rosemont Street, Haverhill,
Massachusetts 01830

Pottery and Ceramic Suppliers with Mail Order Services

American Art Clay Company (AMACO)
4717 W. 16th Street, Indianapolis, Indiana 46222

Denver Fire Clay Company
3033 Blake Street, Denver, Colorado 80205

George Fetzer Company
1205 17th Avenue, Columbus, Ohio 43211

Mohawk Valley Ceramic Supply
221 N. Prospect Street, Herkimer, New York 13350

Seeleys Ceramic Service
9 River Street, Oneonta, New York 13820

Slide Rules

Arthur Brown & Bro., Inc.
2 W. 46th Street, New York, New York 10036

A.I. Friedman, Inc.
25 W. 45th Street, New York, New York 10036

Joseph Mayer Company, Inc.
845 Broadway, New York, New York 10003

Tools

Brodhead-Garrett Company
4560 East 17th Street, Cleveland, Ohio 44105

L.H. Butcher Company
15th and Vermont Streets, San Francisco, California 94103

Craftools, Inc.
401 Broadway, New York, New York 10013

Index

with alumina and silica, 122; table for ratio in formulas, 118; table of basic characteristics, 119
Formula to recipe, procedure for, 49–52
Formulas: for glazes, 48–57; methods of converting, 49–51; molecular, 48–49; of substances used in ceramics, 126–137; tables for converting, 50
Fritting, 42; illus. of, 43

Gases, 23
Geology, 31–34
Glass-formers, 25–27
Glaze materials, sources of, 29–47
Glazes: applying to biscuit-fired ware, 61; applying to unfired ware, 79; calculation of recipes for, 48–57; chemistry of, 13–27; coloring, 97–106; composition in relation to temperature, 55–56; composition of lead, 56; correcting faults in, 79–88; crawling of, 74–75; demonstration of applying, 64–67; devising new, 54–57; fettling, 73; firing, 79–88; firing schedules for, 81–84; formulas for, 48–57; list of pigments for, 100–103; magnified illus. of stoneware, 99, 102; magnified illus. of earthenware, 98; matt turning glossy, 85; methods of applying, 61–68; methods of describing, 48; numbering tests for, 78; opacifiers for, 103; overfiring, 88; 103; painting, 73; parts of, 25–27; peeling and flaking of, 74; pinholing of, 85; preparing, 59–78; preparing clays for, 60; preparing minerals for, 59–60; relationship of composition to color, 57; relationship of composition to surface quality, 56; recipe expressed in percentages, 49; recipe in percentages of weight to oxide, 49; sources of raw materials, 29–47; spraying, 73; table for classification of, 57; table(s) for formula to recipe, 50; table for recipe to formula, 52; table of actual and theoretical percentages of ingredients, 121; table of substances used in, 126–137; testing, 74–78; underfiring 88, weighing out raw materials, 49
Granite: composition of, 34; eruption of, 31; formation of, 31–34; magnified illus. of, 32; pegmatite, 35; table of composition compared to basalt, 34

Iron, reduction firing with, 104

Kiln atmospheres, 103

Leach, Bernard, 34
Lead, 45; conversion of other elements to, 15; geographical distribution of, 47; reduction firing with, 104
Limestone, 40
Liquids, 23; super-cooled, 15
Lustre, 106; illus. of, 105

Materials, distribution of ceramic raw, 47
Metals, 23
Minerals: recipe for weighing out, 49; table of actual and theoretical percentages of, 121
Molecular weights, reference list of, 125

Molecules, accumulation of, 21
Monk at the Potter's Wheel, A, 34

Neutrons, 15

Opacifiers, 103; magnified illus. of glaze containing, 98
Overfiring, 88; illus. of, 86
Orthoclase, 35
Oxides, table of, 27
Oxygen, and a definition of ceramics, 20–21

Painting, 73
Peeling, 84
Periodic table, 116–117
Petalite, 42
Pigments, effects on glaze behavior, 100; from elements, 97–100; list of 100–103
Pinholing, 75
Porcelain, 106
Potter's Book, A, 34
Protons, 15
Pyrometric cones, 27; illus. of, 26; table of recipes from Seger's paper, 123; table of typical compositions, 124

Quartz: illus. of alpha structure, 81; illus. of beta structure, 81

Recipe to formula, procedure for, 52
Recipes: for glazes, 48–57; for weighing out batches, 49
Rocks, formation of sedimentary, 30–31

Salt, 44–45; crystal shape of, 22; illus. of deposits, 41
Seger, Herman, 25–27
Seger cones. *See* pyrometric cones.
Silica, 39; changes in during firing, 80; table for comparison of percentage with flux and alumina, 122; table for ratio in glaze formulas, 118–119
Slide rule: calculating percentages with, 111; dividing with, 109; multiplying with, 109; positioning decimal point of, 109; reading scales of, 106; unifying with, 111–112; using, 107–112
Spraying, 73
Stabilizers, 25–27
Stoneware, 55; reduced, 107; magnified illus. of glaze on, 99

Temperatures, firing, 54–55; relationship to glaze composition, 55–56
Testing, glazes, 74–78; illus. of, 76–77
Trade names, table of, 126–137

Underfiring, 85–88
Unfired ware, applying glazes to, 74

Vapor glazing, 74

Zinc, 45–46; geographical distribution of, 47

Edited by Diane Casella Hines
Designed by James Craig and Robert Fillie
Set in 10 point Times Roman by Harold Black, Inc.
Printed and bound in Japan by Toppan Printing Company, Ltd.